ST/ESA/327

Department of Economic and Social Affairs
Division for the Advancement of Women

Agreed Conclusions of the Commission on the Status of Women on the Critical Areas of Concern of the Beijing Platform for Action 1996-2009

United Nations
New York, 2010

DESA

The Department of Economic and Social Affairs of the United Nations Secretariat is a vital interface between global policies in the economic, social and environmental spheres and national action. The Department works in three main interlinked areas: (i) it compiles, generates and analyses a wide range of economic, social and environmental data and information on which States Members of the United Nations draw to review common problems and to take stock of policy options; (ii) it facilitates the negotiations of Member States in many intergovernmental bodies on joint course of action to address ongoing or emerging global challenges; and (iii) it advises interested Governments on the ways and means of translating policy frameworks developed in United Nations conferences and summits into programmes at the country level and, through technical assistance, helps build national capacities.

Note

The designations employed in this report and the material presented in it do not imply the expression of any opinion whatsoever on the part of the Secretariat of the United Nations concerning the legal status of any country, territory, city or area or of its authorities, or concerning the delimitation of its frontiers or boundaries.

Symbols of United Nations documents are composed of capital letters combined with figures.

This publication has been issued without formal editing.

ISBN 978-92-1-130276-9

UNITED NATIONS PUBLICATION

Sales No. E.09.IV.8

Contents

Introduction

The United Nations Economic and Social Council established the Commission on the Status of Women in June 1946. The Commission reports directly to the Council, and through the Council to the General Assembly. The Commission, which originally had 15 members, grew in several stages to its current size of 45 members. The allocation of seats is based on a formula designed to ensure balanced geographical representation.

In its resolution 11 (II) of 21 June 1946, the Council determined that the Commission would have two basic functions: to prepare recommendations and reports to the Council on "… promoting women's rights in political, economic, civil, social and educational fields," and to make recommendations "… on urgent problems requiring immediate attention in the field of women's rights."

From its establishment in 1946, the mandate of the Commission remained relatively unchanged until 1987, when it was expanded to include advocacy for equality, development and peace. The Commission was also charged with monitoring the implementation of internationally agreed measures for achieving equality between women and men, and reviewing and appraising progress at the national, regional, and global levels.

The Commission meets annually for a period of 10 working days. It stimulates exchange of experience, lessons learned and good practice at the national level, in particular through interactive expert panels. The work of the Commission is supported by the Division for the Advancement of Women, within the United Nations Department of Economic and Social Affairs. The role of the Division is to prepare background documentation, provide substantive servicing of meetings and conferences, assist in the formulation of policy recommendations, and monitor follow-up and implementation of the outcomes of the Commission.

The principal output of the annual sessions of the Commission on the Status of Women is the agreed conclusions on one or more priority themes. Agreed conclusions contain an analysis of achievement of the goals related to the priority themes and a set of concrete policy recommendations. The recommendations, targeting Governments, the United Nations system, other international organizations, civil society actors and other relevant stakeholders, focus on actions to be taken at the international, national, regional and local levels.

Following the Fourth World Conference on Women, held in Beijing, China, in 1995, the General Assembly mandated the Commission to integrate a follow-up process to the Conference into its work programme, regularly reviewing the critical areas of concern of the Beijing Platform for Action, and to develop its catalytic role in mainstreaming gender perspectives in United Nations activities. The Economic and Social Council again modified the Commission's terms of reference in 1996 to include, inter alia, identifying emerging issues, trends and new approaches to issues affecting equality between women and men.

In 1996, on the basis of the outcome of the Fourth World Conference on Women, the Commission adopted a work programme for the years 1996-1999 focused on monitoring the implementation of the Beijing Declaration and Platform for Action.[1] The successive annual sessions of the Commission were devoted to follow-up on the implementation of the 12 critical areas of concern of the Beijing Platform for Action.

Five years after the Fourth World Conference on Women, at its forty-fourth session in February and March 2000, the Commission focused on preparations for the five-year review of implementation of the Beijing Declaration and Platform for Action in the twenty-third special session of the General Assembly, entitled "Women 2000: Gender equality, development and peace for the twenty-first century", in June 2000. The General Assembly adopted by consensus a "Political Declaration"[2] and "Further actions and initiatives to implement the Beijing Declaration and Platform for Action".[3] The outcome documents identified achievements, obstacles and challenges in the implementation of the 12 critical areas of the Platform for Action; and actions and initiatives to overcome obstacles and to achieve the full and accelerated implementation of the Beijing Declaration and Platform for Action.

The Commission developed a multi-year programme of work for the period 2002-2006 at its forty-fifth session, in 2001.[4] This work programme provided a framework for assessing progress in the implementation of the Beijing Platform for Action and the outcome of the special session of the twenty-third special session of the General Assembly.

The 10-year review and appraisal of the implementation of the Beijing Declaration and Platform for Action was carried out by the Commission at its forty-ninth session in 2005. The Commission adopted a declaration in which it reaffirmed the Beijing Declaration and Platform for Action and the

---

[1]   *Report of the Fourth World Conference on Women, Beijing, 4-15 September 1995* (United Nations publications, Sales No. E.96.IV.13) chap. I, resolution 1, annex II.

[2]   General Assembly resolution S-23/2.

[3]   General Assembly resolution S-23/3.

[4]   Economic and Social Council resolution 2001/4.

outcome of the twenty-third special session of the General Assembly and emphasized that full and effective implementation was essential to achieving the internationally agreed development goals, including those contained in the United Nations Millennium Declaration. It called upon all stakeholders to commit themselves fully and to intensify their efforts towards implementation. The declaration also recognized that the Beijing Declaration and Platform for Action and the Convention on the Elimination of All Forms of Discrimination against Women were mutually reinforcing in achieving gender equality and empowerment of women.

At its fiftieth session, in 2006, the Commission revised its methods of work, and decided to focus on one priority theme annually based on the Beijing Platform for Action and the outcome of the twenty-third special session of the General Assembly, with agreed conclusions as the outcome of the consideration of the priority theme. The Commission also decided to evaluate progress annually in the implementation of agreed conclusions from a previous session, and to continue to examine an emerging issue. It adopted a multi-year programme of work for the period 2007-2009.[5] A subsequent multi-year programme for work, covering the period 2010-2014, was agreed upon at the fifty-third session of the Commission in 2009.[6]

The year 2010 marks the fifteenth anniversary of the adoption of the Beijing Declaration and Platform for Action. The Commission accordingly decided to review at its fifty-fourth session the implementation of the Beijing Declaration and Platform for Action and the outcome of the twenty-third special session of the General Assembly, with an emphasis on the sharing of experiences and good practices, so as to overcome remaining obstacles and new challenges, including those related to the Millennium Development Goals.

This volume compiles the agreed conclusions adopted by the Commission between the Fourth World Conference on Women in 1995 and the 15-year review of implementation of the Beijing Declaration and Platform for Action and the outcome of the twenty-third special session of the General Assembly in 2010. While these agreed conclusions focused on various priority themes, a number of overarching issues were consistently highlighted. The importance of gender mainstreaming as a key strategy for achieving gender equality and the empowerment of women was, for example, emphasized in all of the agreed conclusions of the Commission. The agreed conclusions also recognized that the implementation of each critical area would be advanced through the promotion and protection of the human rights of women. The Commission further stressed that a holistic and comprehensive life-cycle approach should be applied to the implementation of all criti-

---

[5]   Economic and Social Council resolution 2006/9.

[6]   Economic and Social Council resolution 2009/15.

cal areas, and has consistently called for the promotion of gender-sensitive research and the development of methodologies for the collection of statistics disaggregated by sex.

The agreed conclusions identified the major obstacles to implementation and the most urgent measures needed to ensure full implementation of each of the critical areas of concern. Among the common challenges to the implementation of all 12 critical areas of concern were, inter alia:

- Limited participation of women in decision-making processes;
- Lack of human and financial resources;
- Persistence of gender stereotypes.

In its agreed conclusions, the Commission also highlighted the need for efficient and close collaboration between all actors: Governments, the United Nations and other international and regional organizations, civil society and the private sector, at the national, regional and international levels, in order to achieve the successful implementation of the Beijing Platform for Action.

The Commission further called on all entities in the United Nations system and the Bretton Woods institutions to contribute to implementation within their respective mandates and to improve coordination at all levels, thereby enhancing the effectiveness of their policies and programmes in support of gender equality and the empowerment of women.

The Beijing Declaration and Platform for Action remain the global policy framework for gender equality and the empowerment of women. The agreed conclusions adopted at the annual sessions of the Commission reaffirm the commitment of Governments to the full implementation of the Beijing Declaration and Platform for Action and the outcome of the twenty-third special session of the General Assembly.

Fortieth session[7]

11-22 March 1996

Resolution:

    40/9.   **Implementation of strategic objectives and action in the critical area of concern: poverty**

Agreed conclusions:

    1996/2.   **Women and the media**

    1996/3.   **Child and dependant care, including sharing of work and family responsibilities**

The agreed conclusions and resolutions adopted for the fortieth session of the Commission on the Status of Women can be found in the *Official Records of the Economic and Social Council, 1996, Supplement No. 6* (E/1996/26-E/CN.6/1996/15).

---

[7]   The Commission considered three priority themes; it adopted a resolution on one of these themes, and agreed conclusions on the other two themes.

Resolution 40/9

Implementation of strategic objectives and action in the critical area of concern: poverty

The Commission on the Status of Women,

Recalling General Assembly resolution 50/203 of 22 December 1995 on the follow-up to the Fourth World Conference on Women,

Recalling also General Assembly resolution 49/110 of 19 December 1994 and other relevant resolutions of the Assembly related to international cooperation for the eradication of poverty in developing countries,

Recalling further Assembly resolution 50/107 of 20 December 1995 on the observance of the International Year for the Eradication of Poverty and proclamation of the first United Nations Decade for the Eradication of Poverty,

Reaffirming the importance of the outcome of the Fourth World Conference on Women held in Beijing from 4 to 15 September 1995, as well as all the United Nations major conferences and summits organized since 1990, in particular the World Summit for Social Development held in Copenhagen in March 1995,

Recognizing that the eradication of poverty will require the implementation and integration of strategies at the national and international levels in all the critical areas of concern in the Platform for Action adopted by the Fourth World Conference on Women,[8]

Taking note of the report of the Secretary-General on poverty[9] in the follow-up to the Fourth World Conference on Women and of the discussion that took place on this issue during the fortieth session of the Commission on the Status of Women,

Reaffirming General Assembly resolutions 50/173 of 22 December 1995 on the United Nations Decade for Human Rights Education, 1995-2004, and 49/184 of 23 December 1994, in which the Assembly expressed the conviction that each woman, man and child, to realize their full human potential, must be made aware of all their human rights and fundamental freedoms, including the right to development,

---

[8] *Report of the Fourth World Conference on Women, Beijing, 4-15 September 1995,* A/CONF.177/20/Rev.1.

[9] E/CN.6/1996/CRP.3.

Recognizing that mainstreaming a gender perspective into all policies and programmes aimed at combating poverty is crucial, as women constitute the majority of people living in poverty,

Recognizing also that the full implementation of the human rights of women and of the girl child, as an inalienable, integral and indivisible part of all human rights and fundamental freedoms, is essential for the advancement of women,

Recognizing further that the commitment of Governments is of fundamental importance in combating poverty and in improving living conditions for women and men,

Recognizing that national and international efforts to eradicate poverty require full and equal participation of women in the formulation and implementation of policies that take fully into account the gender perspective and that empower women to be full partners in development,

Emphasizing that empowering women is a critical factor in the eradication of poverty, since women constitute the majority of people living in poverty and contribute to the economy and to the combating of poverty through both their unremunerated and remunerated work at home, in the community, and in the workplace,

Recognizing that poverty is a global problem affecting all countries and that the complexity of poverty, including the feminization of poverty, requires a wide range of measures and actions, at the national and the regional level, giving particular priority to the situation of women living in poverty and recognizing the need to improve their access to income, education, health care and other resources,

Recognizing also that more women than men live in absolute poverty and that the imbalance is on the increase, resulting in the limited access of women to income, resources, education, health care, nutrition, shelter and safe water in all developing countries, particularly in Africa and in the least developed countries,

Recognizing further that a large number of women in countries with economies in transition are also affected by poverty,

Bearing in mind that the increasing number of women living in poverty in developing countries, both in rural and in urban areas, requires action by the international community in support of actions and measures at the national and regional levels towards the eradication of poverty within the framework of the Beijing Declaration[10] and Platform for Action adopted by the Fourth World Conference on Women,

---

[10]   *Report of the Fourth World Conference on Women ...*

Stressing the necessity of promoting and implementing policies to create a supportive external economic environment, through, inter alia, cooperation in the formulation and implementation of macroeconomic policies, trade liberalization, mobilization and/or the provision of new and additional financial resources that are both adequate and predictable and mobilized in a way that maximizes the availability of such resources for sustainable development, using all available funding sources and mechanisms, enhanced financial stability and ensuring increased access of developing countries to global markets, productive investment and technologies, and appropriate knowledge,

1. *Recognizes* the central role that women play in the eradication of poverty, and stresses the need for their full and equal participation in the formulation and implementation of policies that take fully into account the gender perspective and that empower women to be full partners in development;

2. *Stresses* that the empowerment and autonomy of women and the improvement of women's social, economic and political status are essential for the eradication of poverty and that the full and equal participation of women in decision-making at all levels is an integral part of the process;

3. *Recognizes* that the eradication of poverty is both a complex and a multidimensional issue, and fundamental to promoting equality between men and women as well as to reinforcing peace and achieving sustainable development;

4. *Reaffirms* that the promotion and protection of, and respect for, the human rights and fundamental freedoms of women, including the right to development, which are universal, indivisible, interdependent and interrelated, should be mainstreamed into all policies and programmes aimed at the eradication of poverty, and reaffirms as well the need to take measures to ensure that every person is entitled to participate in, to contribute to and to enjoy economic, social, cultural and political development;

5. *Stresses* that mainstreaming the gender perspective implies examining the ways in which women and men are affected by poverty, the different assets they possess to address the question and their respective contributions and potentials;

6. *Also stresses* that both mainstreaming and other positive actions should be regarded as complementary strategies aimed at enabling the full release of women's and men's development potential and at eradicating poverty;

7. *Urges* all Governments to fulfil their commitments in the Platform for Action to develop, preferably by the end of 1996, national implementation strategies or plans of actions that should also focus on the reduction of overall poverty and on the eradication of absolute poverty, with targets,

benchmarks for monitoring and proposals for allocation or reallocation of resources for implementation, including resources for undertaking gender impact analysis; where necessary the support of the international community could be enlisted, including resources;

8. *Urges* all Governments, the United Nations system, including the Bretton Woods institutions, and civil society, to implement the Platform for Action in its entirety;

9. *Emphasizes* that, in addition to the commitments and recommendations regarding the eradication of poverty outlined in the Programme of Action of the World Summit for Social Development[11] and in the Platform for Action adopted by the Fourth World Conference on Women, specific measures in the Platform for Action should be undertaken to address the feminization of poverty and to mainstream a gender perspective in all policies and programmes for the eradication of poverty, including, inter alia, measures to:

(a) Develop and implement education, training and retraining policies for women and girls;

(b) Undertake legislative and administrative reforms to give women full and equal access to economic resources, including the right to inheritance and to ownership of land and other property, credit, natural resources and appropriate technologies;

(c) Promote the participation of women at all levels of decision-making;

(d) Develop national strategies for promoting employment and self-employment, including entrepreneurial and organizational skills, in order to generate income for women;

(e) Adopt policies to ensure that all women have adequate economic and social protection during unemployment, ill health, maternity, childbearing, widowhood, disability and old age and that women, men and society share responsibilities for child and other dependant care;

(f) Restructure and target the allocation of public expenditures to promote women's economic opportunities and equal access to productive resources and to address the basic social, educational and health needs of women, including access to safe water, particularly of those living in poverty;

(g) Develop gender-based methodologies and conduct research for use in designing more effective policies to recognize and value the

---

[11] *Report of the World Summit for Social Development, Copenhagen, 6-12 March 1995* (A/CONF.166/9), chap. I, resolution 1, annex II.

full contribution of women to the economy through both their unremunerated and renumerated work and to address the feminization of poverty, in particular the relationship between unremunerated work and women's vulnerability to poverty;

(*h*) Develop gender-based methodologies and conduct research to address the contribution of women to the economy, the feminization of poverty, and the economic and social impact of debt and structural adjustment programmes in all developing countries, particularly in Africa and the least developed countries;

(*i*) Analyse, from a gender perspective, macroeconomic and microeconomic policies, and the allocation of public expenditures, which should be designed and implemented with the full and equal participation of women so as to avoid negative impacts on women living in poverty;

(*j*) Reduce excessive military expenditures and investments for arms production and acquisition, as is appropriate and consistent with national security requirements, in order to increase resources for social and economic development;

10. *Calls* for the implementation of the outcome of all other major United Nations conferences and summits related to the eradication of poverty;

11. *Calls upon* States to undertake all commitments of the Copenhagen Declaration on Social Development,[12] taking into account commitments 2 and 5 and the linkages between them, in their efforts to eradicate poverty, and also calls upon all relevant actors to implement promptly the actions and measures for the eradication of poverty, as contained in the Programme of Action of the World Summit for Social Development;[13]

12. *Stresses* the need to fully integrate a gender perspective into the work of all thematic task forces relating to the eradication of poverty established by the Administrative Committee on Coordination, as well as the importance of establishing the proposed inter-agency committee on the follow-up to the Fourth World Conference on Women;

13. *Recommends* that a United Nations system-wide effort be undertaken to review existing indicators, strengthen gender impact analysis of the design and implementation of economic reform programmes, develop complementary, qualitative assessments, and standardize measures and promote their implementation, and stresses that this effort will necessitate effective coordination;

---

[12] Ibid., annex I.

[13] Ibid., annex II, chap. II.

14. *Also recommends* that the secretariats of the United Nations system, including the Bretton Woods institutions, incorporate a coherent method of including both the mainstreaming of the gender perspective and specific gender programmes to achieve equality between women and men in the operational activities, staffing and decision-making spheres of the system;

15. *Stresses* that the United Nations system, including the Bretton Woods institutions, should play a central role in enhancing financial and technical support and assistance for developing countries, particularly African countries and least developed countries, in their efforts to achieve the objectives of the eradication of poverty and the full integration of a gender perspective into all policies and programmes, as set forth in the Beijing Declaration and Platform for Action, particularly the goal of the eradication of poverty;

16. *Recognizes* that the implementation of the Platform for Action in the countries with economies in transition will also require continued international cooperation and assistance, in support of national efforts;

17. *Stresses* the importance of using all available funding sources and mechanisms with a view to contributing towards the goal of poverty eradication and targeting of women living in poverty;

18. *Calls upon* States committed to the initiative of allocation of 20 per cent of official development assistance and 20 per cent of the national budget to basic social programmes to fully integrate a gender perspective into its implementation, as called for in paragraph 16 of General Assembly resolution 50/203;

19. *Invites* all countries, the United Nations system, including the Bretton Woods institutions, relevant international organizations, non-governmental organizations, the private sector, and all other sectors to contribute to the implementation of programmes aimed at eradicating poverty;

20. *Stresses* the need for a coherent and coordinated approach among all partners in development in the implementation of national poverty eradication plans or programmes that fully take into account the gender perspective;

21. *Also stresses* the need for gender-sensitive training, with the assistance of United Nations organizations, of those responsible for the formulation and implementation of development policies and programmes;

22. *Further stresses* the important role of non-governmental organizations as actors involved at the grass-roots level in the policy dialogue designed to reach women through poverty eradication programmes and calls for further efforts to identify ways by which those non-governmental organizations could contribute to the implementation of such programmes;

23.   *Recommends* that the Economic and Social Council, when examining the "Coordination of the activities of the United Nations system for the eradication of poverty" as the theme for the coordination segment of the substantive session of 1996 of the Council, ensure that the relevant organs of the United Nations system take fully into account the gender perspective in their activities for the eradication of poverty, and, likewise, requests that the Council recommend to the General Assembly that the gender dimension of poverty be incorporated into all activities and documentation related to the first United Nations Decade for the Eradication of Poverty;

24.   *Stresses* the need to fully integrate a gender perspective into the coordinated follow-up to major United Nations conferences and summits and recommends that the Economic and Social Council examine, on a regular basis, the extent to which gender factors have been taken into account in the recommendations of all the concerned functional commissions;

25.   *Requests* the Secretary-General to keep in mind the multidimensional nature of poverty in the implementation and review of reports on all other critical areas of concern, taking into consideration the many links between the eradication of poverty and those other critical areas of concern;

26.   *Also requests* the Secretary-General to report on the implementation of the present resolution within the framework of his report on action envisaged to be taken in preparation for the first United Nations Decade for the Eradication of Poverty.

Agreed conclusions 1996/2
Women and the media

1.   The Beijing Platform for Action identifies women and the media as one of 12 critical areas of concern. As stated in the Beijing Platform for Action, gender stereotyping in advertising and the media is one of the factors of inequality that influences attitudes towards equality between women and men. Through a series of dialogues on the subject during its fortieth session, the Commission on the Status of Women examined measures to be used for increasing the participation and access of women to expression and decision-making in and through the media and new technologies of communication. Everywhere the potential exists for the media to make a far greater contribution to the advancement of women. The conclusions emanating from the Commission's dialogue contain proposals for successful implementation of the strategic objectives and actions in the Platform for Action, taking into consideration the importance of implementing all the elements of the Platform.

A.   Respect for the human rights of women, including freedom of expression, and the media

2.   The Commission on the Status of Women reconfirmed the importance it attached to the principles of freedom of expression and of freedom of the press and other means of communication. The Commission discussed freedom of expression from a gender perspective, in particular as it related to women's full enjoyment of freedom of expression, equal access to the media, balanced and diverse portrayals by the media of women and their multiple roles, and media information aimed at eliminating all forms of violence against women. Respect for the human rights of women, including freedom of expression, is a fundamental principle of the international community. In this regard, concern was also expressed about discrimination, threats and acts of violence against professional women in the field of information, including women journalists. If the goal of the full realization of the human rights of women, including freedom of expression, is to be achieved, human rights instruments must be applied in such a way as to take more clearly into consideration the systematic and systemic nature of discrimination against women that gender analysis has clearly indicated.

3.   Relevant United Nations bodies, including the Commission on Human Rights and its mechanisms and procedures, the Committee on the Elimination of Discrimination against Women and independent expert bodies, should within their mandates further examine violations of the human rights of women, including freedom of opinion and freedom of expression, from a gender perspective, in cooperation with the Commission on the Status of Women within its mandate.

B.   Self-regulation, voluntary guidelines and responsiveness to civil society

4.   The Platform for Action states that self-regulatory mechanisms by the media should be encouraged and, consistent with freedom of expression, should include the development of professional guidelines and codes of conduct and other forms of self-regulation so as to eliminate gender-biased programming and to promote the presentation of non-stereotypical images of women and balanced and diverse portrayals of women and men.

5.   In the context of responsiveness to civil society, self-regulation for public and private sector industries should be set within a framework of monitoring, awareness and education and well-developed and effective avenues for complaint. Such self-regulatory measures and voluntary guidelines should be established through a process of dialogue with media professionals, not by coercion.

6. With regard to the presentation of violence in the media, initiatives by Governments and other relevant actors, as appropriate, should be taken to raise awareness of the role of the media in promoting non-stereotyped images of women and men and in eliminating patterns of media presentation that generate violence; to encourage those responsible for media content to establish voluntary professional guidelines and codes of conduct; and to raise awareness also of the important role of the media in informing and educating people about the causes and effects of violence against women.

7. The following initiatives are among those which could be taken, as appropriate, consistent with the freedom of expression:

(a) Encourage the media to take part in international discussions, including the exchange of information and sharing of best practices on voluntary guidelines on a gender-balanced portrayal of women and men. Special attention should be given to the proliferation of transborder and global communications;

(b) Support and encourage women's equal participation in management, programming, education, training and research, including through positive action and equal opportunity policies, with the goal of achieving gender balance in all areas and at all levels of media work, as well as in the media advisory, regulatory and monitoring bodies.

C.   The important role of media education

8. Media education, through, for example, practical workshops and training sessions, is an effective way to create greater awareness of gender stereotyping and equality issues among the general public, government, media industries and professionals.

9. In countries where major parts of the population, including many women, are illiterate or media illiterate, Governments should support the goal of providing appropriate education and training.

10. Civil society at large has an important role in exercising its influence on media content and stereotyped portrayal through consumer action and advocacy and different forms of media watch.

11. At the international level, an exchange of national experiences on media education and other measures can benefit legislators, national broadcasting authorities and media professionals.

D.   Creating an enabling environment

12. The creation of a positive environment is a condition to promote measures intended to achieve a balanced portrayal of women and girls. Changes should be promoted in an enabling way and not through prescrip-

tion. Ongoing research, including the establishment of indicators and monitoring, is important for assessing progress.

13.   An enabling environment should also be created for women's media, including at the international level, such as the development of Womenwatch, a World Wide Web home page to link the United Nations and its activities for women with non-governmental organizations, academics and other users of the Internet. The vital role of non-governmental organizations in media education, research, consumer advocacy and monitoring should be recognized and enhanced.

14.   Media networks should be encouraged to make a commitment or strengthen their commitment to gender equality. Public media, where they exist, should be encouraged to set an example for private media by their commitment and contribution to the advancement of women.

15.   Governments should support research into all aspects of women and the media so as to define areas needing attention and action, and should review existing media policies with a view to integrating a gender perspective.

16.   To the extent consistent with freedom of expression, Governments should take effective measures or institute such measures, including appropriate legislation against pornography and the projection of violence against women and children in the media.

E.   Women and global communications

17.   Advances in information technology have opened up boundaries. The role of women in global communication networks needs to be strengthened. Barriers to such information technology and to women's involvement at every level of its development should be reduced.

Agreed conclusions 1996/3

Child and dependant care, including sharing of work and family responsibilities

1.   Questions relating to child and dependant care, to sharing of family tasks and responsibilities and to unremunerated work must be taken fully into account in mainstreaming a gender perspective, in gender analysis and in all other relevant methodologies used to promote equality between men and women.

2. The main lines of action suggested in order to reduce the burden of family responsibilities on women and bring about the sharing of these responsibilities are set out below.

A. Recognizing change

3. Economic, social and demographic changes—particularly the growing participation of women in economic and social life, the evolving nature of family structures, the feminization of poverty and the link that exists with unremunerated work—and their impact on the capacity of families to ensure the care of children and dependants, as well as the sharing of family responsibilities, including for domestic work, is an issue that affects not only women but society as a whole.

4. As was emphasized in the first plans and strategies drawn up at the national level for the implementation of the Beijing Platform for Action, the sharing of family responsibilities and their reconciliation with professional life must constitute a priority objective.

B. Increasing the role of men in family responsibilities

5. Family responsibilities rest equally with men and with women. Greater participation of men in family responsibilities, including domestic work and child and dependant care, would contribute to the welfare of children, women and men themselves. Even though this change is bound to be slow and difficult, it remains essential.

6. These changes, which imply a change in outlook, can be encouraged by Governments, notably through education and by promoting greater access on the part of men to activities hitherto regarded as women's activities.

C. Changing attitudes and stereotypes

7. It is important to change attitudes towards the status of unremunerated work and the relative role of women and men in the family, the community, the workplace and society at large. Measures taken to this end must be aimed as much at women as at men, and at the different generations, with particular attention to adolescents.

8. These measures should include recognition of the social and economic importance of unremunerated work, and should aim at desegregating the labour market through, inter alia, the adoption and application of laws embodying the principle of equal pay for women and men for equal work or work of equal value.

9. The essential role of the educational system, particularly in primary schools, in changing the perception of the role of girls and boys, must

be recognized. The role of national mechanisms and of non-governmental organizations in promoting change is a major one.

D. Adapting the legal system

10.   There is a need, through legislation and/or other appropriate measures, to rebalance the sharing of family responsibilities between men and women, and to inform them of the existing legislative provisions.

11.   Reconciliation of work-related and family responsibilities and the development of a legislative framework for ensuring child and dependant care (particularly of the elderly and disabled) must be promoted by society as a whole, including social partners, and by Governments. The latter must be the main agents of change.

12.   Action is needed to:

(a) Promulgate and apply laws and other measures to prohibit all forms of direct or indirect discrimination based on gender or matrimonial status, inter alia, by making reference to family responsibilities;

(b) Promote laws on maternity leave;

(c) Promote legislative measures, incentives and/or measures of encouragement that would enable men and women to take parental leave and receive social security benefits. Such measures should protect working men and women against dismissal and guarantee their right to re-enter employment in an equivalent post;

(d) Promote conditions and a way of organizing work that would enable women and men to reconcile their family and professional life, particularly through the introduction of flexi-time for women and men;

(e) Eliminate the differences in remuneration between women and men for equal work or work of equal value, and promote the development of non-discriminatory methods of evaluating work and their inclusion in wage negotiations;

(f) Work actively towards ratification of or accession to and implementation of international and regional human rights treaties;

(g) Ratify and accede to and ensure implementation of the Convention on the Elimination of All Forms of Discrimination against Women so that universal ratification can be achieved by the year 2000;

(h) Ensure the application of laws and guidelines and encourage the adoption of voluntary codes of conduct which guarantee that international labour standards, such as International Labour Organization Convention No. 100 on equality of remuneration of men and women for equal work or work of equal value, apply equally to working women and working men;

(*i*) Encourage the participation of women in bodies responsible for negotiating working conditions. In this respect, it is interesting to note the relationship that exists between the proportion of women participating in negotiations on working conditions and the importance attached to this problem;

(*j*) Encourage social security regimes to take into account the time spent by working men and women on child and dependant care.

E. Adopting and promoting a family support policy and encouraging reconciliation of family and professional life for women and men

13. It is essential to define, at the national, regional and local levels, a family support policy that is based on the principle of equal sharing of family responsibilities and is consistent with the policies for promoting equality in the labour market and protecting the rights of the child. Particular attention should be paid to single-parent families. There is a need, where necessary, to revise legislation so that women are no longer defined as "minors" and/or dependants and to ensure that they enjoy the same access to resources as men.

14. The State and society at large have a responsibility for child and dependant care. This responsibility is reflected in the adoption of an integrated approach at the local and national levels in order to ensure access to affordable and reliable services for the children and dependants (particularly those who are elderly and disabled) of women and men who are working, undergoing training, studying or seeking employment. This responsibility can also take the form of incentives for parents and employers, of a partnership between local authorities, management and labour, non-governmental organizations and the private sector, and of the provision of technical assistance and access to vocational training.

15. With a view to complementing the efforts being made in this direction by Governments, international financial institutions should be encouraged to take into account the growing need for financing to establish day-care nurseries, particularly in areas where there is a greater concentration of poverty, in order to facilitate the training of mothers or their entry into paid employment.

16. Child and dependant care can constitute a major source of new jobs for women and men.

17. The burden of domestic work needs to be eased by making use of appropriate technologies to provide drinking water and an energy supply.

F.   Developing research and information exchange

18.   Research could be conducted drawing on the capabilities of the various United Nations organizations, particularly in the following areas, when compatible with the system-wide medium-term plan for the advancement of women, 1996-2001;

(*a*)   Changes in the situation and attitudes of men and women with regard to the reconciliation of family and professional life and the sharing of family responsibilities—in particular, a study should be conducted in the context of sub-Saharan Africa;

(*b*)   Compilation of data on the unremunerated work which is already taken into account in the System of National Accounts,[14] for example in agriculture and other types of non-mercantile production activity;

(*c*)   Collection and exchange of information on the different systems that exist for alimony payments;

(*d*)   Unremunerated work which addresses the measuring and value of this work, within the framework of the implementation of the Platform for Action;

(*e*)   Time-use surveys of unremunerated work of women and men, with a view to measuring its impact on the use and monitoring of economic and social policies.

G.   Promoting change through international cooperation

19.   The Commission on the Status of Women recommends to the Economic and Social Council that all the strategies and policies of the United Nations and of Member States designed to promote gender equality should take fully into account child and dependant care, sharing of family work and responsibilities between men and women, and unremunerated work, as integral parts of the concept of equality between men and women.

20.   The Commission on the Status of Women recommends to the Economic and Social Council that the suggestions set out above be taken into account in defining the policies of the United Nations system, as well as those of Member States.

---

[14]   United Nations publication, Sales No. E.94.XVII.4.

Forty-first session
10-21 March 1997

Agreed conclusions:

    1997/1.   **Women and the environment**

    1997/2.   **Women in power and decision-making**

    1997/3.   **Women and the economy**

    1997/4.   **Education and training of women**

The agreed conclusions adopted for the forty-first session of the Commission on the Status of Women can be found in the *Official Records of the Economic and Social Council, 1997, Supplement No. 7* (E/1997/27-E/CN.6/1997/9).

Agreed conclusions 1997/1
Women and the environment

1. The recently held United Nations conferences and summits, particularly the Fourth World Conference on Women and the United Nations Conference on Environment and Development, have underlined that the contribution of women to economic development, social development and environmental protection, which are mutually reinforcing components of sustainable development, should be recognized and supported, and that there is need for a clear gender perspective in environmental management. Moreover, unless the contribution of women is recognized and supported, sustainable development will be an elusive goal.

2. In the five-year review and assessment of the results of the United Nations Conference on Environment and Development, moving beyond the concept of women as a major group, a major focus should be the mainstreaming of a gender perspective into the development and implementation of all legislation, policies and programmes, with a view to achieving gender equality, taking into account the Beijing Platform for Action and the results of other global conferences.

3. In designing and implementing environmental programmes and policies, including those related to the implementation of Agenda 21[15] and the Beijing Platform for Action at the national and local levels, all responsible actors should ensure that a gender perspective is fully integrated into them, through the development and application of analytical tools and methodologies for gender-based analysis. Monitoring and accountability mechanisms should be in place to assess gender mainstreaming and its impact.

4. The Commission on Sustainable Development should mainstream a gender perspective into its future work, ensuring that differential impacts on women and men of policies and programmes for sustainable development are well understood and effectively addressed.

5. All responsible actors are requested to adopt a holistic, coordinated and collaborative approach to integrating a gender perspective into sustainable development, between governmental ministries and departments and, at the international level, between United Nations agencies, funds and bodies and other international entities.

6. All responsible actors should support the active participation of women on an equal footing with men in sustainable development at all

---

[15] *Report of the United Nations Conference on Environment and Development, Rio de Janeiro, 3-14 June 1992*, vol. I, *Resolutions Adopted by the Conference* (United Nations publication, Sales No. E.93.I.8 and corrigendum), resolution 1, annex II.

levels, including participation in financial and technical decision-making through appropriate legislation and/or administrative regulations.

7.   Governments should ensure that policies for the liberalization of trade and investment are complemented by effective social and environmental policies into which a gender perspective is fully integrated, so as to ensure that the benefits of growth are fully shared by all sectors of society and to avoid deterioration of the environment.

8.   As consumers, both women and men should be more aware of their ability to behave in an environmentally friendly manner through measures such as eco-labelling that is understood by consumers regardless of age or level of literacy, and local recycling schemes.

9.   Gender-sensitive research on the impact of environmental pollutants and other harmful substances, including the impact on the reproductive health of men and women, should be intensified and linked with the incidence of female cancers. The findings should be widely disseminated, taking into account the results of research on the implementation of national policies and programmes. However, lack of full scientific data should not be a reason for postponing measures that can prevent harm to human health.

10.   The active involvement of women at the national and international levels is essential for the development and implementation of policies aimed at promoting and protecting the environmental aspects of human health, in particular, in setting standards for drinking water, since everyone has a right to access to drinking water in quantity and quality equal to his or her basic needs. A gender perspective should be included in water resource management which, inter alia, values and reinforces the important role that women play in acquiring, conserving and using water. Women should be included in decision-making related to waste disposal, improving water and sanitation systems and industrial, agricultural and land-use projects that affect water quality and quantity. Women should have access to clean, affordable water for their human and economic needs. A prerequisite is the assurance of universal access to safe drinking water and to sanitation, and to that end, cooperation at both the national and international levels should be encouraged.

11.   Governments should combat the illegal export of banned and hazardous chemicals, including agro-chemicals, in accordance with relevant international and regional agreements. Governments should support the negotiation of a legally binding international instrument for the application of prior informed consent procedures for certain hazardous chemicals and pesticides in international trade.

12.   Governments, the international community and international organizations should ensure a participatory approach to environmental protection and conservation at all levels and, in elaborating policies and

programmes, should recognize that sustainable development is a shared responsibility of men and women and should take into account both men's and women's productive and reproductive roles.

13. All Governments should implement their commitments made in Agenda 21 and the Beijing Platform for Action, including those in the area of financial and technical assistance and the transfer of environmentally sound technologies to the developing countries, and should ensure that a gender perspective is mainstreamed into all such assistance and transfers.

14. The international community and United Nations agencies should continue to assist developing countries in developing the capacity to carry out gender impact assessments and in devising analytical tools and gender-sensitive guidelines. A gender perspective should be mainstreamed into all environmental impact assessments. Governments, the private sector and international financial institutions should accelerate efforts to carry out gender impact assessments of investment decisions.

15. Governments, civil society, United Nations agencies and bodies, and other international organizations should collect, analyse and disseminate data disaggregated by sex and information related to women and the environment so as to ensure the integration of gender considerations into the development and implementation of sustainable development policies and programmes.

16. Actors such as the United Nations, international financial institutions, Governments and civil society should apply a gender perspective in all funding programmes for sustainable development, while acknowledging the importance of continuing programming targeted at women. Funds should be shared across sectors.

17. Multilateral and bilateral donors, Governments and the private sector should increase support to non-governmental organizations, particularly to women's organizations, in playing an active role in advocacy for the implementation of Agenda 21 at the international and national levels, particularly in supporting national policies and programmes for sustainable development in the developing countries.

18. Such assistance should also be rendered to the countries with economies in transition at the bilateral and multilateral levels.

19. Governments, educational institutions and non-governmental organizations, including women's organizations, should work in collaboration to provide information on sound environmental practices, support gender-sensitive education and develop specific gender-sensitive training programmes in this area.

20. All relevant actors should be encouraged to work in partnership with adolescent girls and boys, utilizing both formal and non-formal educa-

tional training activities, inter alia, through sustainable consumption patterns and responsible use of natural resources.

21.   Political parties should be encouraged to incorporate environmental goals with a gender dimension into their party platforms.

22.   Governments, in partnership with the private sector and other actors of civil society, should strive to eradicate poverty, especially the feminization of poverty, to change production and consumption patterns and to create sound, well-functioning local economies as the basis for sustainable development, inter alia, by empowering the local population, especially women. It is also important for women to be involved in urban planning, in the provision of basic facilities and communication and transport networks, and in policies concerned with safety. International cooperation should be strengthened to achieve this end.

23.   Women have an essential role to play in the development of sustainable and ecologically sound consumption and production patterns and approaches to natural resource management. The knowledge and expertise of women, especially of rural women and indigenous women, in the use and the protection of natural resources should be recognized, consolidated, protected and fully used in the design and implementation of policies and programmes for the management of the environment.

24.   Laws should be designed and revised to ensure that women have equal access to and control over land, unmediated by male relatives, in order to end land rights discrimination. Women should be accorded secure use rights and should be fully represented in the decision-making bodies that allocate land and other forms of property, credit, information and new technologies. In the implementation of the Beijing Platform for Action, women should be accorded full and equal rights to own land and other property, inter alia, through inheritance. Land reform programmes should begin by acknowledging the equality of women's rights to land and take other measures to increase land availability to poor women and men.

25.   Governments should promote the development of ecological tourism initiatives in order to promote and facilitate women's entrepreneurial activities in this field.

26.   Education and training of young people on the human rights of women should be ensured, and traditional and customary practices that are harmful to and discriminate against women should be eliminated.

27.   Governments, research institutions and the private sector should support the role of women in developing environmentally sound technologies, such as solar energy, and in influencing the development of new and appropriate technologies by ensuring education and training in science and technology.

28.   Governments, the private sector and the international community are called upon to give priority attention to the links between security,

armed conflict and the environment, and their impact on the civilian population, in particular women and children.

29.　Recognizing that gender equality is essential to the achievement of sustainable development, the Chairperson of the Commission on the Status of Women should bring to the attention of the Chairpersons of the Commission on Sustainable Development at its fifth session, and to the General Assembly at its special session to review the implementation of Agenda 21, the agreed conclusions of the Commission on the Status of Women on women and the environment.

Agreed conclusions 1997/2
Women in power and decision-making

1.　Implementation of the Beijing Platform for Action[16] should be accelerated to ensure women's full and equal participation in decision-making at all levels.

2.　Achieving the goal of equal participation of men and women in decision-making and ensuring equal political, economic and social participation of women in all spheres would provide the balance that is needed to strengthen democracy.

3.　Governments and bodies and agencies of the United Nations system, as well as other international organizations, social partners and non-governmental organizations, should collectively and individually accelerate the implementation of strategies that promote gender balance in political decision-making, including in conflict prevention and resolution. They should mainstream a gender perspective, including the use of gender-impact assessments, in all stages of policy formulation and decision-making. They should take into account diverse decision-making styles and organizational practices and take the necessary steps to ensure a gender-sensitive workplace, including a workplace free of sexual harassment and noted for its ability to recruit, promote and retain female staff. Decision-making structures and processes should be improved to encourage the participation of women, including women at the grass-roots level.

4.　Research, including a gender-impact assessment of electoral systems to identify measures that would counter the under-representation of women in decision-making and reverse the downward trend of women in parliaments worldwide, should be supported.

---

[16]　*Report of the Fourth World Conference on Women ...*

5. Political parties are urged to remove discriminatory practices, incorporate gender perspectives into party platforms, and ensure women's access to executive bodies on an equal basis with men, including access to leadership positions as well as to appointed positions and electoral nominating processes.

6. Positive action, including such mechanisms as establishing a minimum percentage of representation for both sexes and/or gender-sensitive measures and processes, is needed to speed the achievement of gender equality and can be an effective policy instrument to improve women's position in sectors and levels where they are underrepresented. All responsible actors in government, the private sector, political parties and non-governmental organizations should review the criteria and processes used in recruitment and appointment to advisory and decision-making bodies, including leadership structures, so as to ensure a comprehensive strategy to achieve gender equality.

7. Governments should commit themselves to establishing the goal of gender balance in decision-making, in administration and public appointments at all levels and in the diplomatic services, inter alia, by establishing specific time-bound targets.

8. Governments and civil society should promote awareness of gender issues and call for their consistent mainstreaming in legislation and public policies.

9. Governments should examine their own communications and policies to ensure the projection of positive images of women in politics and public life.

10. Use of the media both as an image-setting instrument and as a tool to be more effectively used by women candidates should be further explored.

11. Governments, the private sector, political parties, social partners and non-governmental organizations should review the criteria and processes for recruitment and appointment to advisory and decision-making bodies so as to establish the goal of gender balance. At the same time, the business sector should take the challenge to optimize business by promoting a gender balance in the workforce at all levels and to facilitate the reconciliation of work and personal life.

12. Political parties should be encouraged to fund training programmes in conducting campaigns, fund-raising and parliamentary procedures to enable women successfully to run for, be elected to, and serve in public office and parliament. In order to promote reconciliation of work and personal life for women and men, structural changes are needed in the work environment, including flexible working times and meeting arrangements.

13. Governments and the international community should ensure the economic empowerment, education and training of women to enable them to participate in power and decision-making.

14. Governments should promote educational programmes in which the girl child will be prepared to participate in decision-making within the community as a way to promote her future decision-making capacity in all spheres of life.

15. Governments and the United Nations system should promote women's active and equal participation as governmental and non-governmental representatives, special rapporteurs and envoys in all of the initiatives and activities of the system, including as mediators for peace-keeping and peacebuilding.

16. Governments and bodies and agencies of the United Nations system, as well as other international organizations, should actively encourage the sustained participation and equal representation of women and civic movements in all areas, including decision-making processes related to conflict prevention, conflict resolution and rehabilitation, with a view to creating an enabling environment for peace, reconciliation and reconstruction of their communities.

17. Governments and political parties should actively encourage the mainstreaming of a gender perspective in politics and power structures through increasing women's representation in decision-making to a critical mass in both quantitative and qualitative terms. Alternative approaches and changes in institutional structures and practices can contribute significantly to mainstreaming a gender perspective.

18. Governments, political parties and bodies and agencies of the United Nations system, as well as other international organizations and non-governmental organizations, should continue to collect and disseminate data and sex-disaggregated statistics to monitor the representation of women in government at all levels, in political parties, among social partners, in the private sector and in non-governmental organizations at all levels, as well as the participation of women in peace and security.

19. The Secretary-General should ensure full and urgent implementation of the strategic plan of action for the improvement of the status of women in the Secretariat (1995-2000) so as to achieve overall gender equality, in particular at the Professional level and above, by the year 2000. The Consultative Committee on Administrative Questions (Personnel and General Administrative Questions) (CCAQ/PER) should continue to monitor and make concrete recommendations regarding steps being taken in the United Nations Secretariat to achieve the target of 50 per cent women in managerial and decision-making positions by the year 2000, as well as steps to achieve gender balance in the United Nations system as a

whole. Consistent with Article 101 of the Charter of the United Nations, the Secretary-General is urged to increase the number of women employed in the Secretariat from countries that are unrepresented or underrepresented. The Secretary-General should be encouraged to appoint a woman to the proposed new position of Deputy Secretary-General of the United Nations as a step in mainstreaming women in decision-making positions throughout the United Nations system.

20.   International and multilateral agencies should consider ways to communicate and exchange information throughout the United Nations system, inter alia, through the convening of workshops and seminars, including at the managerial level, on best practices and lessons learned for achieving gender balance in institutions, including accountability mechanisms and incentives, and mainstreaming a gender perspective into all policies and programmes, including bilateral and multilateral assistance.

21.   Member States are also encouraged to include women in their delegations to all United Nations and other conferences, including those dealing with security, political, economic, trade, human rights and legal issues, as well as to ensure their representation in all organs of the United Nations and other bodies such as the international financial institutions, where women's participation is negligible.

22.   Member States are urged to promote gender balance at all levels in their diplomatic service, including at the ambassadorial level.

23.   Representation of women from other underrepresented or disadvantaged groups should be promoted by Governments and by bodies and agencies of the United Nations system, as well as other international organizations and non-governmental organizations in decision-making positions and forums.

24.   The attention of Governments is drawn to the general recommendation of the Committee on the Elimination of All Forms of Discrimination against Women on articles 7 and 8 concerning women in public life and decision-making, to be included in the report of the Committee on its seventeenth session.

Agreed conclusions 1997/3
Women and the economy

Governments, international organizations and the private sector should recognize the contributions women make to economic growth through their
paid and unpaid work and as employers, employees and entrepreneurs. They
should adopt the following:

1. Governments, international organizations, the private sector,
non-governmental organizations, social partners (employers' organizations
and labour unions) should adopt a systematic and multifaceted approach to
accelerating women's full participation in economic decision-making at all
levels and ensure the mainstreaming of a gender perspective in the implementation of economic policies, including economic development policies
and poverty eradication programmes. To this end, Governments are urged
to enhance the capacity of women to influence and make economic decisions
as paid workers, managers, employers, elected officials, members of non-
governmental organizations and unions, producers, household managers
and consumers. Governments are encouraged to conduct a gender analysis
of policies and programmes that incorporates information on the full range
of women's and men's paid and unpaid economic activity. Governments,
international organizations, particularly the International Labour Organization (ILO), the private sector and non-governmental organizations,
should develop and share case studies and best practices of gender analysis
in policy areas that affect the economic situation of women.

2. In order to ensure women's empowerment in the economy and
their economic advancement, adequate mobilization of resources at the
national and international levels, as well as new and additional resources to
the developing countries from all available funding mechanisms, including
multilateral, bilateral and private sources, for the advancement of women,
will also be required.

3. Governments should promote and support the elimination of
biases in the educational system so as to counteract the gender segregation
of the labour market, enhance the employability of women, and effectively
improve women's skills and broaden women's access to career choices, in
particular in science, new technologies and other potential and innovative
areas of expansion in terms of employment.

4. Economic policies and structural adjustment programmes, including liberalization policies, should include privatization, financial and trade
policies, should be formulated and monitored in a gender-sensitive way, with
inputs from the women most impacted by these policies, in order to generate positive results for women and men, drawing on research on the gender impact of macroeconomic and micro-economic policies. Governments

should ensure, inter alia, that macroeconomic policies, including financial and public sector reforms, and employment generation, are gender-sensitive and friendly to small-scale and medium-sized enterprises. Local-level regulations and administrative arrangements should be conducive to women entrepreneurs. It is the responsibility of Governments to ensure that women are not discriminated against in times of structural change and economic recession.

5.   Governments should ensure that women's rights, particularly those of rural women and women living in poverty, are being promoted and implemented through their equal access to economic resources, including land, property rights, right to inheritance, credit and traditional savings schemes, such as women's banks and cooperatives.

6.   The international community should actively support national efforts for the promotion of microcredit schemes that ensure women's access to credit, self-employment and integration into the economy.

7.   Microcredit schemes should be supported and monitored in order to evaluate their efficiency in terms of their impact on increasing women's economic empowerment and well-being, income-earning capacity and integration into the economy.

8.   Governments, the private sector and those organizations in civil society that provide training services that promote a gender balance in terms of education and participation in economic activity, should focus on institutional capacity-building and consciousness-raising as well as on improving and upgrading technical skills, including business and management skills and the use of new technologies. Local and traditional technologies and products based on women's knowledge should also be supported and promoted.

9.   Non-governmental organizations and women's organizations should develop incentives for outstanding women entrepreneurs. It is important that Governments, financial institutions, non-governmental organizations, civil society, women's organizations and other relevant actors promote women's entrepreneurial and self-employed activities through technical assistance services or programmes; information on markets; training; the creation of networks, including those at the regional and international levels; and adequate financial support; and, where appropriate, by developing incentives. In order to strengthen the link between sustainable development and poverty eradication, such encouragement and support should extend to businesses owned by women in environmental, resource-based and export-oriented industries.

10.   To secure a critical mass of women's participation in top decision-making positions, Governments should implement and monitor anti-discriminatory laws. The public administration and the private sector should

comply with these laws and introduce changes to corporate structures. Positive or affirmative action can be an effective policy instrument for improving the position of women in sectors and levels of the economy where they are underrepresented. Governments should stimulate employers to introduce objective and transparent procedures for recruitment, gender-sensitive career planning, and monitoring and accountability systems.

11.   Social partners (labour unions and employers' organizations) and non-governmental organizations should consider monitoring and publicizing the enterprises and organizations that take initiatives for the advancement of women and publicizing information on the companies that violate antidiscrimination laws.

12.   Governments should intensify their efforts to implement the actions identified in the Beijing Platform for Action[17] for the elimination of occupational segregation and all forms of employment discrimination. In that regard, the security of women's employment and the conditions for their reintegration into the labour market need to be the subject of special attention. Due consideration should also be given to women in the informal sector and atypical jobs.

13.   Governments, labour unions and the private sector should develop and use analytical tools to compare wages in female and male-dominated occupations, including measures and tools to better reflect the real value of the skills, knowledge and experience of women developed through waged and unwaged work, as well as the full range of the requirements and conditions of waged work, with the aim of achieving equal pay for work of equal value, with a particular focus on minimum wages and low-wage industries. Gender-sensitive monitoring is crucial in enforcing the principle of equal pay for work of equal value. Comprehensive policymaking in this field should include:

(a)   Use of analytical tools;

(b)   Effective legislation;

(c)   Transparency of women's and men's wages;

(d)   Changing the gender-based division of labour and the stereotyped choices of men and women;

(e)   Effective guidance for employers.

14.   Governments are encouraged to develop strategies to increase the well-being of low-waged workers, including enforcement of existing laws in particular in those industries where the most vulnerable workers, predominantly women, are found.

15.   Full integration of women into the formal economy, and in particular into economic decision-making, means changing the current

---

[17]   *Report of the Fourth World Conference on Women ...*

gender-based division of labour into new economic structures where women and men enjoy equal treatment, pay and power. To this end, better sharing of paid and unpaid work between women and men is required. Governments should take or encourage measures, including, where appropriate, the formulation, promotion and implementation of legal and administrative measures to facilitate the reconciliation of work and personal and/or family life, such as child and dependant care, parental leave and flexible working schemes for men and women and, where appropriate, shorter working hours.

16. Governments should consider ratifying the new ILO Convention on home-based workers.

17. Governments and employers should ensure the protection of the rights of migrant women workers, by creating better educational and employment opportunities, preventing and combating trafficking in women and children, and eliminating discrimination against women in the labour market.

18. Governments should monitor and enforce equal opportunity policies and labour laws pertaining to the practices of all of the national and transnational corporations operating in their countries.

19. Women and men should identify and support women-friendly corporations and socially responsible businesses through investments and the use of their services or products.

20. The unpaid work of women, such as work in agriculture, food production, voluntary work, work in family business, and work in natural resource management and in the household, is a considerable contribution to the economy. Unpaid work should be measured and valued through existing and improved mechanisms, including by:

(a) Measuring, in quantitative terms, unremunerated work that is outside national accounts, working to improve methods to assess its value, and accurately reflecting its value in satellite or other official accounts that are separate from but consistent with core national accounts;

(b) Conducting regular time-use studies to measure, in quantitative terms, unremunerated work;

(c) Providing resources and technical assistance to developing countries and countries with economies in transition, in valuing and making visible women's unpaid work.

21. The international community, in particular the creditor countries and international financial institutions, including the Bretton Woods institutions, should further pursue effective, equitable, development-oriented and durable solutions to the external debt and debt-servicing problems of the developing countries on the basis of existing debt relief and reduction mechanisms, including debt reduction, grants and concessional financial

flows, in particular for the least developed countries, taking into account the negative effect of these issues on women and women's programmes.

22. The funds, programmes and specialized agencies of the United Nations system, including the Bretton Woods institutions, and the World Trade Organization, within their respective mandates, should improve coordination and dialogue at all levels, including the field level, in order to ensure the effectiveness of their programmes and policies to support gender equality.

23. Development policies should focus on the economic empowerment of women. The interlinkage between national policies at the macro-level and economic and social gender roles and relations at the micro-level should be clear in order to make the policies more effective. The impact on women of liberalization policies, which include privatization, financial and trade policies, should be assessed.

24. Governments should commit themselves to the goal of gender balance, with special emphasis on reaching a critical mass of women, as soon as possible, when nominating representatives to serve on governing bodies of the organizations of the United Nations system and intergovernmental bodies dealing with policymaking in the areas of finance, economic development, trade and commerce (for example, the Fifth Committee and Second Committee of the General Assembly, the Economic and Social Council, the Trade and Development Board, the Industrial Development Board and the General Council of the World Trade Organization).

25. The production and use of disaggregated statistics by sex should be promoted as a fundamental tool for monitoring the gender division of the labour market and the participation of women in high-level management positions, including economic decision-making, showing the advantages of women's participation in top management and conversely the costs of their exclusion. With regard to the United Nations system, a special data section on women managers should be part of the 1998 synthesis report and the report on the status of the world's women. This could serve as a special mechanism for monitoring how gender-balance goals are being achieved.

26. Issues such as the impact on women of structural adjustment and liberalization policies, which include privatization, financial and trade policies, should be further examined and could be taken up in the context of the report of the Secretary-General on the effective mobilization and integration of women in development, to be considered by the General Assembly at its fifty-second session.

27. The international community, while strengthening international cooperation, should emphasize the importance of an open, rule-based, equitable, secure, non-discriminatory, transparent and predictable multilateral trading system that will also ensure the equal access of women to markets and technologies and resources at both the national and international levels.

Agreed conclusions 1997/4
Education and training of women

1.   There is wide consensus that education and training for girls and women, in particular, provides high social and economic returns and is a precondition for the empowerment of women. Education should be aimed at raising and promoting awareness of the rights of women as human rights. Governments, national, regional and international bodies, bilateral and multilateral donors and civil society, including non-governmental organizations, should continue to make special efforts to reduce the female illiteracy rate to at least half its 1990 level, with emphasis on rural, migrant and refugee women, internally displaced women and women with disabilities, in keeping with the Beijing Platform for Action.[18]

2.   Governments and all other actors should make special efforts to achieve the benchmarks set in the Platform for Action of universal access to basic education and completion of primary education by at least 80 per cent of primary school-age children by the year 2000; close the gender gap in primary and secondary school education by the year 2005; provide universal primary education in all countries before the year 2015; and consider providing multilateral and bilateral assistance.

3.   Governments that have not yet done so should formulate national strategies and action plans for implementation of the Platform for Action that indicate how relevant institutions coordinate action to meet the goals and targets for education. The strategies should be comprehensive, have time-bound targets and benchmarks for monitoring, and include proposals for allocating or reallocating resources for implementation. Mobilization of additional funds from all sources to enable girls and women, as well as boys and men, on an equal basis, to complete their education, may also be necessary.

4.   Donor Governments should strive to meet the agreed target of 0.7 per cent of gross national product for overall official development assistance as soon as possible; and interested developed and developing country partners, having agreed on a mutual commitment to allocate, on average, 20 per cent of official development assistance and 20 per cent of the national budget to basic social programmes, should take into account a gender perspective.

5.   Governments and other actors should promote an active and visible policy of mainstreaming a gender perspective into all policies and programmes, addressing, inter alia, unequal access to educational opportunities and inadequate educational opportunities, and taking into account girls and women in especially difficult circumstances. The education, training

---

[18]   *Report of the Fourth World Conference on Women ...*

and lifelong learning of women should be mainstreamed in policies at all levels, in equal opportunity policies and in national human development plans, where they exist. National machinery for the advancement of women and policymakers in government, employers' organizations, labour unions, non-governmental organizations and the private sector should collaborate to ensure that all policies are responsive to gender concerns and that women and their organizations participate in the policymaking process.

6. Integrated policymaking must highlight the interlinkage between education and training policies, on the one hand, and labour market policies, on the other hand, with an emphasis on the employment and employability of women. In order to enhance the employability of women, basic education and vocational qualifications, in particular in the fields of science and technology, are of great importance. In view of the high presence of women in flexible work-time schemes and atypical work, it is particularly important to facilitate women's participation in "on-the-job training" so that they can secure their jobs and promote their careers.

7. Consciousness should be raised about the need for a new allocation of responsibilities within the family, in order to alleviate the extra burden on women.

8. National statistical offices, responsible governmental ministries, research institutions, women's groups, employers and workers' organizations should provide women, government, policymakers and training providers with the best available labour market information. A redesigned, relevant and up-to-date system of labour market information should provide data disaggregated by sex on training, including employer-sponsored training, present employment trends, income and future employment opportunities.

9. Adult education and training programmes should be developed with a wide focus, incorporating not only literacy and numeracy but also lifelong learning skills and improved capabilities for generating income. Measures should be taken to remove barriers to the participation of women in adult education programmes, such as setting up care structures for children and other dependants.

10. Women who wish to start or improve a microenterprise or small business should have access, not only to financial support services, but also to skills-based training to assist them in the successful management of their business.

11. Governments should meet their responsibilities for providing education and training. Government policies should ensure that different actors in the field of education and training provide and promote equal opportunities for women and men. Governments should promote cooperation among the public and private sectors, including non-governmental organizations, labour unions, employers' organizations and cooperatives, to

make the process of training relevant, efficient and effective. Citizens should help to mobilize governmental and non-governmental efforts, benefiting from the important role that the media can play, to achieve gender equality in education, training and employment. Employers' and workers' organizations should play a critical role in the provision of professional training at the national and local levels. Governments should be ultimately responsible for developing strategies that ensure women's participation in the provision of education and training, especially for women in remote areas or with social, economic, cultural and physical constraints.

12.   Educational planners and policy makers, Governments and other actors should develop programmes in education, technical training and life-long learning that recognize these components as integral parts on a continuum. This implies that knowledge and skills acquired in formal as well as non-formal, out-of-school education, community activities and traditional knowledge are valued and recognized. The programmes should take a holistic approach, ensuring that women enjoy equality throughout the process in a new learning culture involving individuals, enterprises, organizations and society at large.

13.   Educational planners and policymakers should give renewed importance to education in mathematics, science and technology for girls and women. In order to develop the skills required, women need to have full access to education in science and technology at all levels, including the use of modern technologies such as information technology, to vocational training and to lifelong learning. Using a wide range of strategies and modalities, efforts should be made, for instance, through the development of information services and professional guidance for girls and women to promote girls' and women's participation in fields where they are underrepresented, such as science, engineering and technology, and to encourage them to participate actively in the development of new technologies, from design to application, monitoring and evaluation.

14.   The development of gender-sensitive teaching materials, classroom practices and curricula and of awareness-raising and regular gender training for teachers is a prerequisite for breaking down gender stereotypes and developing non-discriminatory education and training aimed at the physical and intellectual development of girls and boys. Teacher training is an essential component in the transmittal of gender-sensitive programmes for eliminating the differential behavioural expectations of girls and boys that reinforce the division of labour by gender. Techniques for improving teachers' capabilities to deliver gender-sensitive instruction need to be researched and widely disseminated in order to support the development of multicultural, gender-sensitive curricula in all areas of instruction.

15.   The recruitment, training, working conditions and the status of teachers, in particular of women teachers, must be improved, and

gender-sensitive training for teachers, teacher trainers, school administrators and planners must be developed. Positive action programmes should be stimulated in order to overcome the under-representation of women in educational management.

16.   The use of instruments available to ensure equality in education and training should be promoted—instruments such as research, information campaigns, refresher courses for teachers, development of gender-sensitive teaching materials, positive action measures and gender-impact assessments. They focus on a variety of actors: girls and boys, parents, teachers, school administrators and policymakers.

17.   Governments should provide increased access to non-discriminatory education and training and create safe, enabling environments in order to retain girls and women in schools and eliminate gender disparities in school attendance at all levels of education, including the higher levels. Safety in schools and during extracurricular activities should be promoted by school authorities, parents and administrative personnel. All actors should join efforts by providing school feeding programmes, transport and boarding schools, when necessary. The contribution of non-governmental organizations to all fields of education and, in particular, to lifelong learning is of importance.

18.   Governments and all actors should recognize the need for and provide gender-sensitive early childhood education, especially to those groups under difficult circumstances, and should assure the lifelong learning of quality education for the girl child.

19.   Governments and all social actors should promote non-formal education programmes and information campaigns to encourage adult women's lifelong learning.

20.   The bodies and specialized agencies of the United Nations system, within their existing mandates, should compile and disseminate information on best practices or strategies for retaining women and girls at all levels of education.

21.   Women's studies should be supported and their curricula and research should be shared among educational institutions and women's organizations to provide role models, publicize women's contributions to their societies' advancement, and develop a foundation for gender-equality education and training.

22.   The Secretary-General, taking into account his overall responsibility for mainstreaming a gender perspective, should continue to analyse and widely disseminate to Governments and non-governmental organizations, through *Women 2000* and other publications in the official United Nations languages, information on the education and training of women and girls as part of the follow-up to the Fourth World Conference on Women.

Forty-second session
2-13 March 1998

Agreed conclusions:

    1998/I.   **Violence against women**

    1998/II.   **Women and armed conflict**

    1998/III.   **Human rights of women**

    1998/IV.   **The girl child**

The agreed conclusions adopted for the forty-second session of the Commission on the Status of Women can be found in the *Resolutions and decisions adopted by the Economic and Social Council at its substantive session of 1998* (E/1998/INF/3/Add.2), resolution 1998/12.

Agreed conclusions 1998/I
Violence against women

The Commission on the Status of Women

Reaffirms the Beijing Platform for Action,[19] notably chapter IV.D on violence against women, the Convention on the Elimination of All Forms of Discrimination against Women,[20] and the Declaration on the Elimination of Violence against Women;[21]

Requests States parties to the Convention on the Elimination of All Forms of Discrimination against Women to take into account in their initial and periodic reports to the Committee on the Elimination of Discrimination against Women general recommendation 19 on violence against women, adopted by the Committee at its eleventh session,[22] and the Declaration on the Elimination of Violence against Women;

Requests States parties to international human rights treaties to compile information and report on the extent and manifestations of violence against women, including domestic violence and harmful traditional practices, and the measures taken to eliminate such violence, for inclusion in reports under the Committee on the Elimination of Discrimination against Women, and to include such information in reports to other treaty bodies;

Proposes, in order to accelerate the implementation of the strategic objectives of chapter IV.D:

A.   An integrated, holistic approach

Actions to be taken by Governments and the international community

- Formulate comprehensive, multidisciplinary and coordinated national plans, programmes or strategies, which will be widely disseminated, to eliminate all forms of violence against women and girls and provide for targets, timetables for implementation and effective domestic enforcement procedures by monitoring mechanisms, involving all parties concerned, including consultations with women's organizations;
- Call upon the international community to condemn and act against all forms and manifestations of terrorism, in particular those that affect women and children;
- Develop strong and effective national, regional and international cooperation to prevent and eliminate trafficking in women and girls, espe-

---

[19]   *Report of the Fourth World Conference on Women* ...

[20]   General Assembly resolution 34/180, annex.

[21]   General Assembly resolution 48/104.

[22]   See *Official Records of the General Assembly, Forty-seventh Session, Supplement No. 38* (A/47/38), chap. I.

cially for purposes of economic and sexual exploitation, including the exploitation of prostitution of women and girls;

- Encourage the media to take measures against the projection of images of violence against women and children;

- Strengthen effective partnerships with non-governmental organizations and all relevant agencies to promote an integrated and holistic approach to the elimination of violence against women and girls;

- Integrate effective actions to end violence against women into all areas of public and private life, as a means of working to overcome the violence and discrimination that women face because of such factors as race, language, ethnicity, poverty, culture, religion, age, disability and socio-economic class or because they are indigenous people, migrants, including women migrant workers, displaced women or refugees;

- Ensure that comprehensive programmes for the rehabilitation of victims of rape are integrated into global programmes.

B. Provision of resources to combat violence against all women

Actions to be taken by Government, non-governmental organizations and the public and private sector, as appropriate

- Support the work of non-governmental organizations in their activities to prevent, combat and eliminate violence against women;

- Provide adequate resources for women's groups, helplines, crisis centres and other support services, including credit, medical, psychological and other counselling services, as well as focus on vocational skill training for women victims of violence that enables them to find a means of subsistence;

- Provide resources for the strengthening of legal mechanisms for prosecuting those who commit acts of violence against women and girls, and for the rehabilitation of victims;

- Support and encourage partnerships for the establishment of national networks and provide resources for shelters and relief support for women and girls, so as to offer a safe, sensitive and integrated response to women victims of violence, including the provision of programmes designed to heal victims of trafficking and rehabilitate them into society;

- Consider increasing contributions for national, regional and international action to combat violence against women, including for the Special Rapporteur of the Commission on Human Rights on violence against women, its causes and consequences and the Trust Fund in Support of Action to Eliminate Violence against Women of the United Nations Development Fund for Women;

- Develop special programmes that would assist women and girls with disabilities in recognizing and reporting acts of violence, including the provision of accessible support services for their protection and safety;
- Encourage and fund the training of personnel in the administration of justice, law enforcement agencies, security, social and health-care services, schools and migration authorities on matters related to gender-based violence, and its prevention, and the protection of women from violence;
- Include in national budgets adequate resources related to the elimination of violence against women and girls.

C. Creation of linkages and cooperation with regard to particular forms of violence against women

Actions to be taken by Governments

- Consider, where appropriate, formulating bilateral, subregional and regional agreements to promote and protect the rights of migrant workers, especially women and girls;
- Develop bilateral, subregional, regional and international agreements and protocols to combat all forms of trafficking in women and girls, and assist victims of violence resulting from prostitution and trafficking;
- Improve international information exchange on trafficking in women and girls by recommending the setting up of a data-collection centre within Interpol, regional law enforcement agencies and national police forces, as appropriate;
- Strengthen the implementation of all relevant human rights instruments in order to eliminate organized and other forms of trafficking in women and girls, including trafficking for the purpose of sexual exploitation and of pornography;
- Strengthen gender focal points of the regional commissions, and further enhance their contributions to gender-balanced development policies, as they have already made significant contributions by helping Member States to build capacities and as regards gender-mainstreaming for alleviating gender-based violence against women, and have contributed actively to promoting the human rights of women.

D. Legal measures

Actions to be taken by Governments

- Ensure the gender-sensitive development of an integrated framework that includes criminal, civil, evidentiary and procedural provisions and that addresses sufficiently the multiple forms of violence against women;

- Take all appropriate measures to develop an integrated and comprehensive legislative framework that addresses sufficiently the multiple forms of violence against women;

- Promote, where necessary, the harmonization of local legislation that penalizes acts of violence against women;

- Provide adequate infrastructure and support services to respond to the needs of the survivors of violence against women and girls, and to assist towards full recovery and reintegration into society, such as witness protection programmes, restraining orders against perpetrators, crisis centres, telephone hotlines, shelters, provisions for economic support and livelihood assistance;

- Develop guidelines to ensure appropriate police and prosecutorial responses in cases of violence against women;

- Establish and support programmes that provide legal aid and assistance for women and girls bringing complaints relating to gender-based violence through various applicable ways and means, such as non-governmental organization support for women with claims relating to violence against women;

- Ensure the accountability of relevant law enforcement agencies for implementation of policies to protect women from gender-based violence;

- Investigate, and in accordance with national legislation, punish all acts of violence against women and girls, including those perpetrated by public officials;

- Implement strategies and practical measures, taking account of the Model Strategies and Practical Measures on the Elimination of Violence against Women in the Field of Crime Prevention and Criminal Justice adopted by the General Assembly, in its resolution 52/86 of 12 December 1997, and contained in the annex thereto;

- Review national legislation in order to effect complete legal prohibition of rape and all forms of violence against women and girls, such as domestic violence, including rape, and to ensure that legislation that protects women and girls from violence is effectively implemented;

- Criminalize all forms of trafficking in women and girls for the purposes of sexual exploitation and penalize all traffickers;

- Take steps to enable women who are victims of trafficking to make complaints to the police and to be available when required by the criminal justice system, and ensure that during this time women have access to social, medical, financial and legal assistance, and protection, as appropriate;

- Develop and implement national legislation and policies prohibiting harmful customary or traditional practices that are violations of women's and girls' human rights and obstacles to the full enjoyment by women and girls of their human rights and fundamental freedoms;

- Ensure that women are safe at work by supporting measures that promote the creation of a workplace environment free from sexual harassment or other violence and encourage all employers to put in place policies designed to eliminate and deal effectively with harassment of women whenever it occurs in the workplace;
- Encourage the participation of women in law enforcement agencies so as to achieve gender balance.

E. Research and gender-disaggregated data collection

Actions to be taken by Governments

- Promote coordinated research on violence against women to ensure that it is multidisciplinary and addresses the root factors, including external factors, that encourage trafficking in women and girls for prostitution and other forms of sexual exploitation;
- Encourage research aimed at exploring the nature, extent and causes of violence and collect data and statistics on its economic and social costs, and its consequences, and conduct research on the impact of all laws relevant to combating all forms of violence against women;
- Develop common definitions and guidelines and train relevant actors for the collection of data and statistics on violence against women and ensure that all cases of violence against women are recorded systematically and appropriately, whether they are first reported to the police or to health and social services;
- Sponsor community-based research and national surveys, including the collection of disaggregated data, on violence against women, with regard to particular groups of women, such as women with disabilities, migrant women workers and trafficked women;
- Support evaluations of the impact of measures and policies, particularly with regard to legislative, evidentiary and procedural law reform, to address violence against women with a view to identifying and exchanging good practices and lessons learned, and initiate intervention and prevention programmes;
- Promote the sharing of research results, including information on best practices at national, regional and international levels;
- Explore the possibility of mechanisms such as national rapporteurs, who report to Governments on the scale, prevention and combating of violence against women, particularly trafficking in women and girls.

Action to be taken by the United Nations

- Consider ways to share good practices and lessons learned, including establishing a readily accessible database of good practices and lessons learned with regard to all forms of violence against women.

F.   Change attitudes

Actions to be taken by Governments and civil society, including non-governmental organizations

- Work to create violence-free societies by implementing participatory educational programmes on human rights, conflict resolution and gender equality, for women and men of all ages, beginning with girls and boys;

- Support programmes of peer mediation and conflict resolution for schoolchildren and special training for teachers to equip them to encourage cooperation and respect for diversity and gender;

- Encourage innovative education and training in schools to enhance awareness of gender-based violence by promoting non-violent conflict resolution, and short-, mid- and long-term strategic educational goals for achieving gender equality;

- Introduce and invest in comprehensive public awareness campaigns, such as "zero tolerance", that portray violence against women as unacceptable;

- Encourage the promotion in media portrayals of positive images of women and of men, presenting them as cooperative and full partners in the upbringing of their children, and discourage the media from presenting negative images of women and girls;

- Encourage the media to create positive images of women and men as cooperative and crucial actors in preventing violence against women through the development of voluntary international media codes of conduct, on positive images, portrayals and representations of women, and on the coverage of the reporting of violence against women;

- Raise awareness and mobilize public opinion to eliminate female genital mutilation and other harmful traditional, cultural or customary practices that violate the human rights of women and girls and negatively affect their health;

- Promote the responsible use of new information technologies, in particular the Internet, including the encouraging of steps to prevent the use of these technologies for discrimination and violence against women, and for trafficking in women for the purposes of sexual exploitation, including the exploitation of prostitution of women and girls;

- Create policies and programmes to encourage behavioural change in perpetrators of violence against women, including rape, and monitor and assess the impact and effect of such programmes;

- Establish legal literacy programmes to make women aware of their rights and the methods of seeking protection under the law;

- Recognize that women and girls with disabilities, women migrants and refugee women and girls could be particularly affected by violence, and encourage the development of programmes for their support;
- Encourage campaigns aimed at clarifying opportunities, limitations and rights in the event of migration so as to enable women to make informed decisions and to prevent them from becoming victims of trafficking;
- Encourage and support men's own initiatives to complement efforts of women's organizations to prevent and eliminate violence against women and girls;
- Conduct research on, and create policies and programmes to change, the attitudes and behaviour of perpetrators of violence against women within family and society;
- Actively encourage, support and implement measures aimed at increasing the knowledge and understanding of violence against women, through gender analysis capacity-building and gender-sensitive training for law enforcement officers, police personnel, the judiciary, medical and social workers, and teachers.

Agreed conclusions 1998/II
Women and armed conflict

The Commission on the Status of Women

Reaffirms the Beijing Platform for Action,[23] notably chapter IV.E on women and armed conflict;

Proposes the following, taking into account the Commission's conclusions on human rights of women, violence against women and the girl child, in order to accelerate the implementation of the strategic objectives of chapter IV.E:

A. Ensuring gender-sensitive justice

Actions to be taken by Governments

- Ensure that national legal systems provide accessible and gender-sensitive avenues of redress for victims of armed conflict;

---

[23] *Report of the Fourth World Conference on Women ...*

- Ensure that a gender-sensitive perspective is integrated in the drafting and interpretation of international law and domestic legislation, including for the protection of women and girls in armed conflict;

- Support efforts to create an international criminal court that integrates a gender perspective in its statute and functioning, enabling a gender-sensitive interpretation and application of the statute;

- Provide and disseminate to the public in local languages, including to women's groups and non-governmental organizations, information on the jurisdiction and procedures for accessing the ad hoc war crimes tribunals, human rights treaty bodies and all other relevant mechanisms; this information should be widely and actively disseminated in cooperation with the United Nations system and non-governmental organizations;

- Protect children in situations of armed conflict, especially the girl child, against participation, recruitment, rape and sexual exploitation through adherence to the applicable principles of international human rights law, international humanitarian law and national legislation;

- Promote a gender balance and gender expertise in all relevant international bodies, at all times, including the International Law Commission, the ad hoc war crimes tribunals and the human rights treaty bodies, having due regard for the principle of equitable geographical distribution;

- Examine and consider modifying existing legal definitions and standards to ensure that they encompass concerns of all women and girls affected by armed conflict and, in particular, reaffirm that rape, systematic rape and sexual slavery in armed conflict constitute war crimes;

- Ensure that where crimes of sexual violence are committed in situations of conflict, all perpetrators, including those among United Nations and international peacekeeping and humanitarian personnel, are prosecuted.

B. Specific needs of women affected by armed conflict

Actions to be taken by Governments and international organizations

- Collect and provide information on violations of the human rights of women under foreign occupation and take steps to ensure the full enjoyment of the human rights of these women;

- Take account of the impact of armed conflict on the health of all women and introduce measures to address the full range of women's health needs, including those of women with disabilities, and the psychological needs arising from trauma stemming from sexual abuses and the effects of violations of their rights;

- Address the specific needs and concerns of women refugees and displaced persons and ensure appropriate training for relevant bodies to address the specific needs and concerns of women refugees, who should receive special protection, including the proper design and location of camps and the adequate staffing of camps;

- Recognize the importance of fully involving women in designing rehabilitation policies in post-conflict situations and take steps to assist household economies, including the social and economic conditions of women-headed households and widows;

- Ensure the physical safety and security of all refugee women and girls and those internally displaced by, inter alia, adequately providing for and increasing their access to the right of return to their country or place of origin, and the participation of women in the committees responsible for the management of camps, and ensure that the camps are designed in accordance with the 1995 Guidelines on the Protection of Refugee Women[24] of the United Nations High Commissioner for Refugees; and arrange for gender-sensitive legal, social and medical services in camps, and for the talents and capabilities of refugee and displaced women and girls to be fully integrated in the development and implementation of these programmes while they are in such camps;

- Provide refugee victims of sexual violence and their families with adequate medical and psychosocial care, including culturally sensitive counselling, and ensure confidentiality;

- Take measures in accordance with international law with a view to alleviating any negative impact of economic sanctions on women and children;

- Mainstream a gender perspective, as appropriate, into national immigration and asylum policies, regulations and practices, in order to extend protection to those women whose claim for protection is based on gender-related persecution;

- Provide and strengthen assistance to all women and girls in conflict and post-conflict situations, including through non-governmental organizations, as appropriate. Refugee women and men must have equal rights in the administration and distribution of goods and services in the camps;

- Condemn and bring to an immediate end massive violations of human rights, especially in the form of genocide, and ethnic cleansing as a strategy of war, and its consequences, such as rape, including systematic rape of women in war situations;

---

[24] Geneva, United Nations High Commissioner for Refugees, 1995.

- Encourage rehabilitation centres to ensure that the knowledge and professions of displaced and refugee people are utilized;
- Mainstream a gender perspective into humanitarian responses to crises and armed conflicts and into post-conflict reconstruction activities.

C. Increasing the participation of women in peacekeeping, peacebuilding, pre- and post-conflict decision-making, conflict prevention, post-conflict resolution and reconstruction

Actions to be taken by Governments and international and regional intergovernmental institutions

- Increase, including through measures of affirmative action, women's participation and leadership in decision-making and in preventing conflict;
- Mainstream a gender perspective into peace-promoting activities at all levels as well as humanitarian and peacebuilding policies, including through gender analysis and the encouragement of the participation of more female personnel at all levels, in particular at senior or high levels in field missions, and monitor and review such policies as appropriate, on the basis of equitable geographical distribution where applicable;
- Recognize and support women's non-governmental organizations, particularly at the grass-roots level, in respect of their preventing conflict, including early warning and peacebuilding;
- Take note of the Kampala Action Plan on Women and Peace,[25] as well as the post-Beijing follow-up Kigali Declaration on Peace, Gender and Development,[26] and the Plan of Action for Conflict-affected Areas,[27] and, if appropriate, convene conferences to assess progress and promote implementation;
- Regional research and training institutes should carry out research on the role of women in conflict resolution and identify and analyse policies and action programmes;
- Create mechanisms to encourage more women candidates with the appropriate qualifications to apply for judicial, prosecutorial and other positions in all relevant international bodies, in order to achieve gender balance on the basis of equitable geographical distribution;

---

[25]   Document E/ECA/ATRCW/ARCC.XV/94/7, April 1994.

[26]   A/52/720, annex, sect. 4.

[27]   Ibid., sect. 3.

- Nominate and appoint more women as special representatives in conflict resolution, taking due consideration of the principle of equitable geographical distribution;

- Enhance the role of women in bilateral preventive diplomacy efforts as well as those undertaken by the United Nations in accordance with the Charter of the United Nations;

- Ensure that the participants in humanitarian missions and in peacekeeping operations, both military and civilian, are given specific gender-sensitive training;

- Develop and implement innovative strategies to increase the participation of women in peacekeeping operations and invite the Secretary-General to analyse their effectiveness in his reports on peacekeeping operations, if appropriate, based on an expert group meeting;

- Mainstream a gender perspective into bilateral and multilateral peacebuilding discussions and promotion of social development.

D. Preventing conflict and promoting a culture of peace

Actions to be taken by Governments the international community

- Integrate a gender perspective into foreign policies and adjust policies accordingly;

- Support the establishment of women-for-peace networks;

- Discourage the adoption of and refrain from any unilateral measure that is not in accordance with international law and the Charter of the United Nations and that impedes the full achievement of economic and social development by the population of the affected countries, in particular women and children, that hinders their well-being and that creates obstacles to the full enjoyment of their human rights;

- Ensure that education, including teacher training, promotes peace, respect for human rights and gender-sensitivity, tolerance for diversity, including cultural and religious diversity, and pluralism;

- Encourage the incorporation of relevant international humanitarian law principles and their interpretation from a gender perspective into national legal systems;

- Encourage and support the participation of young people in programmes, seminars and workshops on conflict resolution and human rights, negotiations for the peaceful settlement of disputes and the importance of a gender perspective in the promotion of a culture of peace, development and human rights of women;

- Strengthen ongoing efforts to train international peacekeeping forces on human rights and gender sensitivity and provide training on codes of conduct and prevention of violence against women, ensuring that trainers include civilians, women and experts in gender issues;

- Enhance the culture of peace and the peaceful settlement of armed conflicts, including through mass media, audio and video, as appropriate;

- Draw upon and utilize the expertise of the Office of the United Nations High Commissioner for Refugees, the United Nations High Commissioner for Human Rights, the Division for the Advancement of Women of the United Nations Secretariat, the United Nations Development Fund for Women and the United Nations Children's Fund for the preparation of materials for the training of United Nations peacekeepers;

- Continue to make resources available nationally and internationally for prevention of conflict and ensure women's participation in the elaboration and implementation of strategies for preventing conflict;

- Recognize and support the work done by national machineries for the advancement of women and by non-governmental organizations and work towards mobilizing the action necessary to encourage the achievement by women of a critical mass at the national cabinet level in key ministries and departments and in international organizations that make or influence policy with regard to matters related to collective peace and security.

Actions to be taken by the United Nations

- Acknowledge and support the vital work of non-governmental organizations in the field of peace in efforts towards preventing conflict and for peacebuilding;

- Organize programmes and seminars to sensitize community leaders and women on the important role that women should play in developing a culture of peace in society.

E. Disarmament measures, illicit arms trafficking, landmines and small arms

Actions to be taken by Governments:

- In order to alleviate the suffering of women and children caused by landmines, work towards the objective of eliminating anti-personnel landmines; and in this regard take due note of the conclusion of the Convention on the Prohibition of the Use, Stockpiling, Production and Transfer of Anti-personnel Mines and on Their Destruction and its implementation by those States that become parties to it;

- Join international efforts to elaborate international policies to prohibit illicit traffic, trade and transfer of small arms, and to control their excessive production, with a view to alleviating the suffering of women and children in the situation of armed conflict;

- Provide landmine awareness campaigns or classes in close coopera-tion with communities and community leaders formally and infor-mally, making them accessible to women in afflicted areas, and provide resources and assistance for landmine clearance and share technology and information so that local populations can engage effectively in the safe clearance of landmines;

- Support programmes for the rehabilitation and social integration of women victims of anti-personnel landmines, and demining and mine awareness activities;

- Encourage as appropriate the role of women in the peace movement, working towards general and complete disarmament under strict and effective international control including disarmament of all types of weapons of mass destruction;

- Work to prevent and put an end to aggression and all forms of armed conflict, thereby promoting a culture of peace.

Agreed conclusions 1998/III
Human rights of women

The Commission on the Status of Women

Reaffirms the Beijing Platform for Action adopted by the Fourth World Conference on Women,[28] in particular chapter IV.I on the human rights of women, and the Vienna Declaration and Programme of Action adopted by the World Conference on Human Rights;[29]

Recommends that the Commission on Human Rights give particular attention to the economic and social rights of women in any discussions it may have at its fifty-fourth session on the question of the appointment and mandate of a special rapporteur on economic, social and cultural rights, or a specific aspect thereof; and invites the Secretary-General to report to the Commission on the Status of Women in 1999 on decisions taken by the Commission on Human Rights on this issue, and further recommends that the rapporteur on economic, social and cultural rights, if appointed, should make his or her reports available to the Commission on the Status of Women;

[28] *Report of the Fourth World Conference on Women ...*
[29] A/CONF.157/24 (Part I), chap. III.

Proposes, in order to accelerate the implementation of the strategic objectives of chapter IV.I of the Platform for Action:

A. Creation and development of an environment conducive to women's enjoyment of their human rights and awareness-raising

Actions to be taken by Governments, non-governmental organizations, employers, trade unions, the private sector and other actors in civil society, as appropriate

- Ensure universal awareness by all persons, women and men, girls and boys of all human rights and fundamental freedoms of women and children, including the girl child, through comprehensive human rights education in accordance with the United Nations Decade for Human Rights Education, and create and promote a culture of human rights, development and peace;

- Encourage and support broad-based national and community-based dialogues that include women and men, and girls and boys, from diverse backgrounds, on the meaning of human rights, on the obligations thereby created and on gender-specific discrimination and violations;

- Ensure that work, including, inter alia, work by treaty bodies within their mandates to develop an understanding of the gender dimensions of human rights, is compiled and widely disseminated, and that this gender-sensitive interpretation of human rights is fully integrated into all policies and programmes of international and regional organizations;

- Make widely available reports of United Nations mechanisms that deal with the human rights of women, such as on discrimination and violence against women, to the public, including the judiciary, parliamentarians and non-governmental organizations;

- Support, encourage and disseminate research, and collect gender- and age-disaggregated statistics on factors and multiple barriers that affect the full enjoyment by women of their economic, social, cultural, civil and political rights, including their right to development, and on violations that are particular to women, and disseminate the findings and utilize the collected data in assessing the implementation of the human rights of women;

- Develop and implement national legislation and policies prohibiting customary and traditional practices that are harmful to women and that are violations of women's human rights;

- Eradicate customary or traditional practices, particularly female genital mutilation, that are harmful to, or discriminatory against, women and that are violations of women's human rights and fundamental freedoms, through the design and implementation of awareness-raising programmes, education and training;

- Ensure that their personnel periodically receive gender training and are educated and made aware of all women's, men's and children's human rights;

- Mobilize the resources necessary and create the conditions for the full exercise of women's economic, social, cultural, civil and political rights;

- Establish and strengthen partnerships and cooperation with each other and with the United Nations system and regional organizations in order to promote more actively the full enjoyment by women of their human rights;

- Ensure that indigenous and other marginalized women's special conditions are taken fully into consideration within the framework of the human rights of women;

- Mainstream a gender perspective, as appropriate, into national immigration and asylum policies, regulations and practices in order to extend protection to those women whose claim for protection is based on gender-related persecution.

B. Legal and regulatory framework

Actions to be taken by Governments

- Guarantee the existence of a national legal and regulatory framework, including independent national institutions, or other appropriate mechanisms, that ensure the full realization of all human rights of women and girls on the basis of equality and non-discrimination, including their right to be free from violence, in accordance with the Charter of the United Nations, other instruments related to human rights and international law;

- Take steps, including a gender-sensitive review of national legislation, to revoke any laws or legal procedures and eradicate practices—national or customary—that promote discrimination on the basis of sex;

- Ensure that women and children have full and equal access to effective legal remedies for violations, including domestic mechanisms, which are monitored and revised to ensure that they function without discrimination, and international mechanisms that address human rights as provided, inter alia, under the Convention on the Elimination of All Forms of Discrimination against Women;[30]

---

[30] General Assembly resolution 34/180, annex.

- Promote changes that ensure that women enjoy equal opportunities in law and in practice to claim their rights through national legal systems, including through educating them on these rights as well as ensuring availability of measures such as free or affordable legal aid, legal representation and court appeals procedures, and support existing programmes of non-governmental organizations and other agencies.

C. Policies, mechanisms and machineries

Actions to be taken by Governments

- Ratify and accede to and ensure implementation of the Convention on the Elimination of All Forms of Discrimination against Women[31] so that universal ratification of the Convention can be achieved by the year 2000;

- Limit the extent of any reservations to the Convention on the Elimination of All Forms of Discrimination against Women; formulate any such reservations as precisely and as narrowly as possible; ensure that no reservations are incompatible with the object and purpose of the Convention or otherwise incompatible with international treaty law and regularly review those reservations with a view to withdrawing them; and withdraw reservations that are contrary to the object and purpose of the Convention or that are otherwise incompatible with international treaty law;

- Create channels of communication to promote information exchange between national institutions that address the human rights of women and non-governmental organizations and relevant policy-making bodies of Government;

- Create gender mainstreaming mechanisms within all policy-making bodies so that women's ability to enjoy their rights is strengthened by all policies and programmes, including through gender-sensitive budgeting;

- Support efforts to create an international criminal court that integrates a gender perspective in its statute and functioning, enabling a gender-sensitive interpretation and application of the statute;

- Mainstream a gender perspective into all economic and social policies in order to promote the human rights of women and girls, including their right to development;

- Adopt measures to ensure by appropriate means that women enjoy equal opportunities to participate in decision-making processes, including parliamentary and other elected assemblies.

---

[31]   Ibid.

Actions to be taken by States parties to human rights instruments

- Promote gender balance in the nomination and election of independent experts to treaty bodies having expertise and sensitivity in regard to gender issues in the field of human rights, giving due consideration to equitable geographical distribution and different legal systems;

- Take note of the report of the United Nations Secretariat to the Committee on the Elimination of Discrimination against Women on reservations to the Convention on the Elimination of All Forms of Discrimination against Women[32] and encourage similar studies by other treaty bodies, as well as by the Sixth Committee of the General Assembly, especially with respect to their effect on women's and girls' enjoyment of their human rights;

- Ensure that their periodic reports to treaty monitoring bodies mainstream a gender perspective.

Within the United Nations system

- Urge the Commission on Human Rights to ensure that all human rights mechanisms and procedures fully incorporate a gender perspective in their work, within their respective mandates;

- The Administrative Committee on Coordination Inter-Agency Committee on Women and Gender Equality should, as planned, conduct a workshop to clarify the understanding of a rights-based approach to women's empowerment and advancement and to gender equality, drawing on the work already being done in this regard by the United Nations Development Fund for Women and others;

- The Office of the United Nations High Commissioner for Human Rights and the Division for the Advancement of Women of the Department of Economic and Social Affairs of the United Nations Secretariat should strengthen and improve coordination in general human rights activities within their respective mandates and continue to prepare the joint annual work plan;

- The Office of the United Nations High Commissioner for Human Rights and the Division for the Advancement of Women should continue to prepare the joint annual work plan and strengthen cooperation and coordination in human rights activities, in particular:

  (a) By collaborating in the writing of reports for the Commission on the Status of Women and the Commission on Human Rights, the first initiative of this type[33] being welcomed;

---

[32] CEDAW/C/1997/4.

[33] E/CN.4/1998/22E/CN.6/1998/11.

(*b*) Through sharing information systematically on the Committee on the Elimination of Discrimination against Women, its sessions and documentation, in order to ensure that its work will be better integrated into the work of the other treaty bodies and United Nations human rights activities;

(*c*) Through capacity-building to implement agreed conclusions 1997/2 of the Economic and Social Council[34] on mainstreaming a gender perspective into all policies and programmes in the United Nations system, in particular training and gender sensitization; especially of human rights monitors;

- Take further steps to increase cooperation and promote integration of objectives and goals among the Commission on the Status of Women, the Commission on Human Rights and the Committee on the Elimination of Discrimination against Women, as well as the United Nations Development Fund for Women, the International Research and Training Institute for the Advancement of Women, the United Nations Development Programme, the United Nations Children's Fund and other United Nations funds and programmes;

- Cooperation, communication and exchange of expertise should be enhanced between the Commission on the Status of Women and other functional commissions of the Economic and Social Council, including the Commission on Human Rights, in order to more effectively promote women's human rights;

- The treaty bodies within their mandates should continue to promote a better understanding of the rights contained in international human rights instruments and their particular significance to women;

- Given the importance of general comments in clarifying the provisions of human rights treaties, the Committee on the Elimination of Discrimination against Women is invited to draw up joint general comments with other treaty bodies, within their respective mandates, on the universality, indivisibility, interdependence and interrelatedness of human rights and should discuss these and other collaborative activities at the annual chairpersons meeting;

- The treaty bodies should continue to develop working methods that facilitate communications between non-governmental organizations, treaty bodies and the States parties;

- The Office of the United Nations High Commissioner for Human Rights is commended for establishing a gender team for studying, within the mandate of the Office, the human rights of women; the team should be given the necessary support by the most senior levels of management and decision-making to carry out its work effectively;

---

[34]   See A/52/3, chap. IV, sect. A, para. 4.

- Specialized agencies and other bodies of the United Nations system, as well as other international financial and national trade organizations, should develop innovative ways of integrating the promotion of women's enjoyment of their human rights in all their policies and programmes.

Agreed conclusions 1998/IV
The girl child

The Commission on the Status of Women

Reaffirms the Beijing Platform for Action adopted by the Fourth World Conference on Women,[35] notably chapter IV.L on the girl child, the Vienna Declaration and Programme of Action adopted by the World Conference on Human Rights,[36] the Convention on the Elimination of All Forms of Discrimination against Women[37] and the Convention on the Rights of the Child;[38]

Proposes, in order to accelerate the implementation of the strategic objectives of chapter IV.L:

A. Promotion and protection of the human rights of the girl child

Actions to be taken by Governments, local authorities, non-governmental organizations and civil society and the United Nations system, as appropriate

- Promote further the enjoyment by children, particularly the girl child, of their human rights, by the elaboration of an optional protocol to the Convention on the Rights of the Child on measures for the prevention and eradication of the sale of children, child prostitution and pornography;
- Organize community-based actions, including the setting up of local committees to create awareness of, and monitor conformity with, the Convention on the Rights of the Child and the Convention on the Elimination of All Forms of Discrimination against Women, with a special focus on the situation of adolescent girls and young mothers;

---

[35] *Report of the Fourth World Conference on Women* ...

[36] A/CONF.157/24 (Part I), chap. III.

[37] General Assembly resolution 34/180, annex.

[38] General Assembly resolution 44/25, annex.

- Conduct awareness-raising campaigns designed to mobilize communities, including community leaders, religious organizations, parents and other family members, especially male family members, with regard to the rights of the child, giving special emphasis to the girl child, and monitor changes in attitudes;

- Conduct awareness-raising campaigns and gender training targeted at law enforcement and justice system officials with regard to the rights of children, giving special attention to the girl child;

- Eliminate traditional and customary practices that constitute son-preference through awareness-raising campaigns and gender training;

- Recognize and promote the contribution of girls and boys to development;

- Promote non-discriminatory treatment of girls and boys in the family and, in this regard, adopt measures to ensure equal access by girls and boys to food, education and health.

Actions to be taken by States parties to the Convention on the Rights of the Child and the Convention on the Elimination of All Forms of Discrimination against Women

- Include comprehensive information and sex- and age-disaggregated data on children in their reports to the Committee on the Rights of the Child and the Committee on the Elimination of Discrimination against Women, and invite the treaty monitoring bodies to pay special attention to the rights of the girl child while assessing those reports;

- Ensure that any reservations to the Convention on the Elimination of All Forms of Discrimination against Women and the Convention on the Rights of the Child are formulated as precisely and as narrowly as possible and that they are not incompatible with the object and purpose of those conventions, and review the reservations to the Convention on the Elimination of All Forms of Discrimination against Women and the Convention on the Rights of the Child with a view to withdrawing them.

B. Education and empowerment of the girl child

Actions to be taken by Governments, educational institutions and the United Nations system, as appropriate

- Consider drawing upon the findings and recommendations of the United Nations Expert Group Meeting on Adolescent Girls and Their Rights, held in Addis Ababa in October 1997;

- Consider making primary education compulsory;

- Ensure universal enrolment and retention of girls in school and ensure the continued education of pregnant adolescents and young mothers in order to guarantee basic education to the girl child;
- Encourage all levels of society, including parents, Governments and non-governmental organizations, to support the implementation of educational policies to enhance gender awareness in the community;
- Provide gender-sensitive training for school administrators, parents and all members of the school community, such as local administrators, staff, teachers, school boards and students;
- Review teaching materials, including textbooks, to promote the self-esteem of women and girls through positive self-images and revise these materials, highlighting women's effective role in society, including in decision-making, development, culture, history, sports and other social, political and economic endeavours;
- Develop programmes of sensitization on the gender perspective for staff of government offices working on educational issues concerning indigenous and rural girls, and develop educational materials adapted to their situation;
- Identify the special needs of girls in difficult circumstances, including girls from migrant families, refugee and displaced girls, girls from ethnic minorities, indigenous girls, orphaned girls, girls with disabilities and other girls with special needs, and provide the resources necessary to address their needs;
- Involve girls, including girls with special needs, and their representative organizations in the decision-making process and include them as full and active partners in identifying their own needs and in designing, planning, implementing and assessing policies and programmes to meet those needs;
- Provide training opportunities for girls to develop their skills in leadership, advocacy and conflict resolution;
- Make visible girls' and boys' unpaid work in the household by conducting research and documenting gender differences, particularly in rural communities, note the implications of household work for girls' equal access to basic and further education and career development and take measures to redress imbalances and eliminate discrimination.

C. Health needs of girls

Actions to be taken by Governments, civil society and the United Nations system, as appropriate

- Protect the girl child from all forms of sexual exploitation and sexual abuse by taking appropriate measures, including, for example, designing and implementing legislation;

- Encourage parents, coalitions of concerned organizations and individuals, especially political leaders, popular and community figures and the media, to advocate for children's health, including adolescent girls' reproductive and sexual health;

- Eradicate all customary or traditional practices, particularly female genital mutilation, that are harmful to or discriminate against women and girls and that are violations of women's human rights and obstacles to the full enjoyment by women of their human rights and fundamental freedoms, through the design and implementation of awareness-raising programmes, education and training, as well as programmes to help the victims of such practices to overcome their trauma;

- Develop and implement national legislation and policies prohibiting customary or traditional practices that are violations of women's human rights and obstacles to the full enjoyment by women of their human rights and fundamental freedoms and prosecute the perpetrators of practices that are harmful to the health of women and girls;

- Make widely available information and counselling to adolescent girls and boys, especially on human relationships, reproductive and sexual health, sexually transmitted diseases and adolescent pregnancy, that are confidential and easily accessible and emphasize the equal responsibility of girls and boys;

- Improve the health care for adolescent girls by health personnel and provide the latter with appropriate training, and encourage health-care personnel to work with girls to understand their special needs;

- Recognize and protect from discrimination pregnant adolescents and young mothers and support their continued access to information, health care, nutrition, education and training;

- Support the activities of non-governmental organizations in the area of reproductive health and health orientation centres for girls;

- Enact laws concerning the minimum age for marriage and raise the minimum age for marriage when necessary in order to ensure respect for the rights of the child, as stipulated in the Convention on the Rights of the Child.[39]

D. Girls in armed conflict

Actions to be taken by the United Nations and Governments

- Incorporate information on the rights of the child in the mandates and operational guidelines of peacekeeping forces, the military and humanitarian workers and provide them with gender-sensitive training;

---

[39] General Assembly resolution 44/25, annex.

- Encourage girls and other individuals and communities to play a key role in reporting violations of rights of girls in armed conflict to the appropriate authorities and ensure adequate, accessible and gender-sensitive support services and counselling;

- Protect the girl child in situations of armed conflict against participation in armed conflicts, recruitment, rape and sexual exploitation, in particular through the adoption of an optional protocol to the Convention on the Rights of the Child,[40] as recommended by the General Assembly;

- Take measures to address the special needs of girls for protection and for gender-appropriate support and counselling centres in refugee camps, and in resettlement and reintegration efforts;

- Create and respect zones of peace for children in armed conflict.

E. Trafficking, including for purposes of prostitution and other forms of sexual exploitation

Actions to be taken by Governments, international organizations and civil society

- Collect information and raise public awareness on the issue of trafficking, physical and psychological abuse, and sexual exploitation of girls in order to better design and improve preventive programmes;

- Consider implementing the recommendations of the Declaration and Agenda for Action of the World Congress against Commercial Sexual Exploitation of Children,[41] held in Stockholm in 1996;

- Establish recovery programmes for children who have been abused or sexually exploited, with specially trained personnel to provide a safe and supportive environment.

Actions to be taken by Governments

- Enact and enforce laws that prohibit sexual exploitation, including prostitution, incest, abuse and trafficking of children, paying special attention to girls;

- Prosecute and punish persons and organizations engaged in and/or promoting the sex industry, sexual exploitation, acts of paedophilia, trafficking in organs, child pornography and sex tourism involving minors, and condemn and penalize all those offenders involved, whether local or foreign, while ensuring that children who are victims of those practices are not penalized;

---

[40]   Ibid.

[41]   A/51/385, annex.

- Design mechanisms and strengthen international cooperation to better protect girls and bring to justice the perpetrators of such crimes;
- Adopt measures that ensure that judicial and legal processes are sensitive to the specific needs of abused girls to prevent further traumatization or victimization.

F.   Labour and the girl child

Actions to be taken by Governments, international organizations and the private sector

- Consider ratifying and implementing international agreements that are designed to protect children, including conventions of the International Labour Organization, and bring national legislation into conformity with those agreements in order to protect the girl child;
- Ensure that girls who work have access to education and vocational training, health, food, shelter and recreation on equal and favourable conditions, and are protected from economic exploitation, sexual harassment and abuse in the workplace;
- Pay special attention to girls in the informal sector, such as domestic workers, and develop measures to protect their human rights and fundamental freedoms and prevent their economic exploitation, ill-treatment and sexual abuse;
- Raise government and public awareness as to the nature and scope of the special needs of girls employed as domestic workers and of those performing excessive domestic chores in their own households, and develop measures to prevent their economic exploitation and sexual abuse;
- Actively contribute to efforts at the 1998 session of the International Labour Conference to draw up a new international convention to eliminate the most abhorrent forms of child labour;
- Consider the implementation of the actions identified in the Agenda for Action[42] of the 1997 Oslo Conference on Child Labour.

G.   General recommendations

Actions to be taken by Governments and the United Nations system

- Prepare programmes for the girl child as part of national action plans in order to fully implement the Beijing Platform for Action adopted by the Fourth World Conference on Women;[43]

---

[42]   A/53/57.

[43]   *Report of the Fourth World Conference on Women ...*

- The organizations of the United Nations system, in particular the United Nations Children's Fund, as the agency mandated to deal with the rights and concerns of children, should give greater attention to the girl child through Fund country programmes, using its goodwill ambassadors for raising awareness on the situation of the girl child on national, regional and international levels;

- The Secretary-General should report on the girl child to the Commission on the Status of Women prior to the five-year review of the implementation of the Beijing Platform for Action;

- Base programmes and policies for the girl child on the rights of the child, the responsibilities, rights and duties of the parents and the evolving capacity of the girl child, in accordance with the Beijing Platform for Action and the Convention on the Rights of the Child.[44]

---

[44] General Assembly resolution 44/25, annex.

Forty-third session
1-12 March and 1 April 1999

Agreed conclusions:

    1991/I.   **Women and health**

    1999/II.   **Institutional mechanisms**

The agreed conclusions adopted for the forty-third session of the Commission on the Status of Women can be found in the *Resolutions and decisions adopted by the Economic and Social Council at the 10th meeting of its resumed organizational session for 1999 and at its substantive session of 1999* (E/1999/INF/2/Add.2), resolution 1999/17.

Agreed conclusions 1999/I
Women and health

The Commission on the Status of Women

1. *Reaffirms* the Beijing Platform for Action, adopted by the Fourth World Conference on Women,[45] notably chapter IV.C on women and health, the Programme of Action of the International Conference on Population and Development[46] and the Convention on the Elimination of All Forms of Discrimination against Women;[47]

2. *Recalls* the Constitution of the World Health Organization, which states that health is a state of complete physical, mental and social well-being and not merely the absence of disease or infirmity; that the enjoyment of the highest attainable standard of health is one of the fundamental rights of every human being without distinction of race, religion, political belief, economic or social condition; and that the health of all peoples is fundamental to the attainment of peace and security and is dependent upon the fullest cooperation of individuals and States;

3. *Requests* States parties to the Convention on the Elimination of All Forms of Discrimination against Women to consider, when preparing their initial and periodic reports under the Convention, including on article 12, general recommendations of the Committee on the Elimination of Discrimination against Women;

4. *Acknowledges* that the realization by women of their right to the enjoyment of the highest attainable standard of physical and mental health is an integral part of the full realization by them of all human rights, and that the human rights of women and of the girl child are an inalienable, integral and indivisible part of universal human rights;

5. *Acknowledges* the link between women's physical and mental health throughout the life cycle and the level of national development, including the availability of basic social services such as health services, women's status and degree of empowerment in society, employment and work, poverty, illiteracy, ageing, race and ethnicity, and violence in all its forms, in particular harmful attitudes and traditional or customary practices affecting the health of women, as well as the importance of investing in women's health for the well-being of women themselves and for the development of society as a whole;

---

[45] *Report of the Fourth World Conference on Women* ...

[46] *Report of the International Conference on Population and Development, Cairo, 5-13 September 1994* (United Nations publication, Sales No. E.95.XIII.18), chap. I, resolution 1, annex.

[47] General Assembly resolution 34/180, annex.

6.   *Recognizes* that lack of development is a major obstacle for women in many countries and that the international economic environment, through its impact on national economies, affects the capacity of many countries to provide and expand quality health services to women; further significant obstacles include competing governmental priorities and inadequate resources;

7.   *Proposes*, in order to accelerate the implementation of the strategic objectives of chapter IV.C of the Beijing Platform for Action, that the following actions be taken:

Actions to be taken by Governments, the United Nations system and civil society, as appropriate

1.   *Universal access, on a basis of equality between women and men, to quality, comprehensive and affordable health care and health services and information by women throughout the life cycle*

   (a)   Ensure universal access on a basis of equality between women and men to appropriate, affordable and quality health care and health services for women throughout the life cycle;

   (b)   In order to bridge the gap between commitments and implementation, formulate policies favourable to investments in women's health and intensify efforts to meet the targets identified in the Platform for Action;

   (c)   Ensure universal access for women throughout the life cycle, on a basis of equality between women and men, to social services related to health care, including education, clean water and safe sanitation, nutrition, food security and health education programmes;

   (d)   Integrate sexual, reproductive and mental health services, with emphasis on preventative measures, within the primary health-care system to respond to the broad health needs of women and men, in a life-cycle approach;

   (e)   Design and implement programmes, with the full involvement of young people, to educate and inform them on sexual and reproductive health issues, taking into account the rights of the child to access to information, privacy, confidentiality, respect and informed consent, and the responsibilities, rights and duties of parents and legal guardians;

   (f)   Allocate and reallocate, where appropriate, adequate resources to put in place the necessary measures which ensure that quality health services are accessible to those women throughout their life cycle who are living in poverty, are disadvantaged or socially excluded;

(g) Increase efforts directed towards poverty eradication, by assessing the impact of broader macroeconomic policies on the feminization of poverty and on women's health; and address the health needs of those vulnerable, throughout their life span;

(h) Adopt preventive and promotional health policies at an early stage where possible in order to prevent health problems and dependence of older women and enable them to lead independent and healthy lives;

(i) Ensure that special attention is given to supporting women with disabilities, and empower them to lead independent and healthy lives;

(j) Address the need for appropriate screening services for women, within the context of national health priorities;

(k) Encourage women to practise regular sport and recreational activities which have a positive impact on women's health, well-being and fitness throughout the whole life cycle, and ensure that women enjoy equal opportunities to practise sport, use sport facilities and take part in competitions.

2. *Sexual and reproductive health*

(a) Accelerate efforts for the implementation of the targets established in the Beijing Platform for Action with regard to universal access to quality and affordable health services, including reproductive and sexual health, reduction of persistently high maternal mortality and infant and child mortality and reduction of severe and moderate malnutrition and iron deficiency anaemia,[48] as well as to provide maternal and essential obstetric care, including emergency care, and implement existing and develop new strategies to prevent maternal deaths, caused by, inter alia, infections, malnutrition, hypertension during pregnancy, unsafe abortion[49] and post-partum haemorrhage, and child deaths, taking into account the Safe Motherhood Initiative;

(b) Promote and support breastfeeding unless it is medically contraindicated, as well as implement the International Code of Marketing of Breast-milk Substitutes and the Baby Friendly Hospital Initiative;

(c) Support scientific research into and the development of safe, affordable, effective and easily accessible female-controlled methods of family planning, including dual methods such as micro-

---

[48] *Report of the Fourth World Conference on Women ...*, para. 106 (w).

[49] Ibid., para. 106 (k).

bicides and female condoms that protect against both sexually transmitted diseases and human immunodeficiency virus/ acquired immunodeficiency syndrome (HIV/AIDS) and prevent pregnancy, taking into account paragraph 96 of the report of the Fourth World Conference on Women;

(d) Support the development and widespread use of male contraceptive methods;

(e) Educate women and men, particularly young people, with a view to encouraging men to accept their responsibilities in matters related to sexuality, reproduction and child-rearing and to promoting equal relationships between women and men;

(f) Enhance women's ability and knowledge, and empower them to make informed choices, to prevent unwanted pregnancies;

(g) Work with the media and other sectors to encourage the development of positive attitudes about major transitions in women's and girls' reproductive lives, such as the onset of menstruation and menopause, and provide appropriate support, where needed, for women undergoing these transitions;

(h) Eradicate the practice of female genital mutilation, and other harmful traditional and customary practices affecting the health of women and girls, since such practices constitute a definite form of violence against women and girls and a serious form of violation of their human rights, including through development of appropriate policies and enactment and/or reinforcement of legislation, and ensure development of appropriate tools of education and advocacy and adopt legislation outlawing their practice by medical personnel;

(i) Take all necessary measures to prevent all harmful practices, such as early marriages, forced marriages and threats to women's right to life.

3. *HIV/AIDS, sexually transmitted diseases and other infectious diseases*

(a) Support public education and advocacy and secure the highest level of political commitment to the prevention of and research into sexually transmitted diseases and HIV/AIDS, their care, treatment and the mitigation of their impact, including through the provision of social services and support, together with poverty alleviation;

(b) Increase prevention measures to reduce the spread of the HIV/ AIDS pandemic worldwide and sexually transmitted diseases among the groups most heavily at risk, in particular young people, including through education and awareness-raising campaigns and improved access to high-quality condoms and improved accessibility to anti-retroviral therapy to prevent mother-to-child transmission of HIV, and treatment, care and support for HIV/AIDS-related illnesses;

(*c*) Enact laws and take measures to eliminate sexual violence against women and girls, which is one of the causes of HIV/AIDS infection and other sexually transmitted diseases, and review and enact laws and combat practices, as appropriate, that may contribute to women's susceptibility to these infections, including enacting legislation against those sociocultural practices that contribute to AIDS, and implement legislation, policies and practices to protect women, adolescents and young girls from discrimination related to HIV/AIDS;

(*d*) Eliminate the stigmatization and social exclusion that surround HIV/AIDS, sexually transmitted diseases and other infectious diseases such as leprosy and filariasis, and lead to under-detection, lack of treatment and violence, especially for women, so that infected women who reveal their HIV status are protected from violence, stigmatization and other negative consequences;

(*e*) Increase the preventive, as well as the therapeutic, measures against tuberculosis and malaria, and accelerate the research into the development of a vaccine against malaria, which has a harmful effect especially on pregnant women in most parts of the world, particularly in Africa;

(*f*) Educate, counsel and encourage men and women infected with HIV/AIDS and sexually transmitted diseases to inform their partners to help protect them from infection, and ensure that the spread of these diseases is curtailed.

4. *Mental health and substance abuse*

(*a*) Make available gender-sensitive and age-sensitive mental health services and counselling, as necessary, with particular attention to the treatment of psychiatric illness and trauma throughout the life cycle, inter alia, by integrating them into primary health-care systems and through appropriate referral support;

(*b*) Develop effective preventive and remedial health services to provide appropriate counselling and treatment for mental disorders related to stress, depression, powerlessness, marginalization and trauma since women and girls may suffer more from these ailments resulting from various forms of discrimination, violence and sexual exploitation, particularly in situations of armed conflict and displacement;

(*c*) Support research and dissemination of information on gender differences in the causes and effects of the use and abuse of substances, including narcotic drugs and alcohol, and develop effective gender-sensitive approaches to prevention, treatment and rehabilitation, including those specifically designed for pregnant women;

(d) Design, implement and strengthen prevention programmes aimed at reducing tobacco use by women and girls; investigate the exploitation and targeting of young women by the tobacco industry; support action to prohibit tobacco advertising and access by minors to tobacco products; and support smoke-free spaces, gender-sensitive cessation programmes, and product labelling to warn of the dangers of tobacco use, noting the Tobacco Free Initiative proposed by the World Health Organization in July 1998;

(e) Promote equitable sharing of household and family responsibilities between women and men, and provide social support systems, where appropriate, to help women who, as a result of their multiple roles in the family, often may suffer from fatigue and stress;

(f) Support research on the relationship between women's and girls' physical and mental health, self-esteem and the extent to which women of all ages are valued in their societies to address issues such as substance abuse and eating disorders.

5. *Occupational and environmental health*

(a) Support for gender-specific research on the short- and long-term effects of the occupational and environmental health risks of work, including work in the formal and informal sectors, performed by both women and men, and take effective legal and other measures to reduce these risks, including risks in the workplace, in the environment and from harmful chemicals, including pesticides, radiation, toxic waste and other such hazards that affect women's health;

(b) Protect the health of women workers in all sectors, including agricultural and domestic household workers, through effective environmental and occupational health policies for gender-sensitive work environments, free from sexual harassment and discrimination, which are safe and ergonomically designed to prevent occupational hazards;

(c) Take specific measures to protect the health of women workers who are pregnant or have recently given birth or are breastfeeding from harmful environmental and occupational hazards, and their children;

(d) Provide full and accurate information about environmental health risks to the public, in particular to women, and take steps to ensure access to clean water, adequate sanitation and clean air.

6.   *Policy development, research, training and evaluation*

   (*a*)   Advance a comprehensive interdisciplinary and collaborative research agenda on women's health which encompasses the entire life span of all women, including women from special and diverse groups within populations;

   (*b*)   Establish concrete accountability mechanisms at the national level for reporting on the implementation of the health and other related critical areas of the Platform for Action;

   (*c*)   Improve the collection, use and dissemination of data disaggregated by sex and age, and research findings, and develop collection methodologies that capture the differences between women's and men's life experiences, including through the use and, where necessary, further coordinated development of gender-specific qualitative and quantitative health indicators that go beyond morbidity, mortality and social indicators, capturing quality of life, and the social as well as mental well-being of women and girls;

   (*d*)   Promote research on the interrelationship between poverty, ageing and gender;

   (*e*)   Ensure participation of women at all levels in the planning, implementation and evaluation of health programmes; ensure also a gender perspective in the health sector at all levels, including through the elaboration of gender- and age-sensitive health policies and budgets, and the creation of an enabling environment supported by a legislative framework and monitoring, follow-up and evaluation mechanisms within individual countries;

   (*f*)   Mainstream a gender perspective into the curricula as well as the training of all health-care and service providers in order to ensure high-quality health services for women that can help eliminate discriminatory attitudes and practices by certain health professionals which impede women's access to health services; and ensure that a gender perspective is developed and applied to treatment and prevention practice in the health sector;

   (*g*)   In order to ensure that women's rights are addressed, the curricula of health-care providers should include relevant human rights topics to strengthen medical ethics and ensure that girls and women are treated with respect and dignity;

   (*h*)   Increase education and research among health service providers and users to address the unnecessary medicalization of women's health conditions;

   (*i*)   Ensure, where indicated, that clinical trials of pharmaceuticals, medical devices and other medical products include women with their full knowledge and consent and ensure that the resulting data is analysed for sex and gender differences;

(*j*)   Collect data concerning scientific and legal developments on human genome and related genetic research and their implications for women's health and women's rights in general and disseminate such information and results of studies conducted in accordance with accepted ethical standards.

7.   *Health sector reform and development*

(*a*)   Take action, in the context of health sector reform and development and growing diversification of the provision of care, to secure equal and equitable access to care for women and to ensure that health sector reform and development efforts promote women's health; and address under-provision of health care;

(*b*)   Take the opportunity provided by health sector reform and development to systematically integrate the process of gender analysis in the health sector and undertake gender impact assessments and monitoring of all health sector reforms and development to ensure that women benefit equally from them;

(*c*)   Develop strategies designed to seek to reduce occupational concentration by gender to eliminate gender-based pay inequality, to ensure high-quality working conditions in the health workforce, and to provide appropriate skills training and development.

8.   *International cooperation*

(*a*)   Assure a strong political commitment by the international community to implement strengthened international cooperation for development and to mobilize domestic and international finance resources from all sources for development and the provision of health services for women;

(*b*)   Promote progress in regard to external debt relief which, with improvement in the terms of trade, could help generate resources, both public and private, to expand and upgrade health services, with special attention to the physical and mental health of women;

(*c*)   Encourage the international community, including bilateral donors and multilateral development organizations, to assist developing countries in ensuring the provision of basic social services, including health-care services for women, in particular during periods of economic difficulty; socially and gender-sensitive approaches to structural adjustment policies are further encouraged;

(*d*) Encourage concerted efforts, through enhanced cooperation and coordination to minimize the negative impacts and maximize the benefits of globalization and interdependence, to enhance, inter alia, the provision of health-care services in developing countries, especially for women;

(*e*) In the framework of international cooperation, encourage sound macroeconomic policies and institutions to support, inter alia, the provision of health-care services for women.

Agreed conclusions 1999/II
Institutional mechanisms

The Commission on the Status of Women

1. *Reaffirms* the Beijing Platform for Action, adopted by the Fourth World Conference on Women,[50] notably chapter IV.H on institutional mechanisms for the advancement of women, the Convention on the Elimination of All Forms of Discrimination against Women[51] and Economic and Social Council agreed conclusions 1997/2 on mainstreaming the gender perspective into all policies and programmes in the United Nations system;[52]

2. *Recognizes* that the effectiveness and sustainability of national machineries are highly dependent on their embeddedness in the national context, the political and socio-economic system and the needs of and accountability to women, including those with the least access to resources; in addition, recognizes that sharing information at the regional and international levels is crucial for strengthening national machineries and other related institutional mechanisms; that gender equality is advanced through the promotion and protection of all human rights and fundamental freedoms, respect for democracy, peace and development; and that the full involvement of women and men is essential;

3. *Further recognizes* that gender mainstreaming is a tool for effective policymaking at all levels and not a substitute for targeted, women-specific policies and programmes, equality legislation, national machineries for the advancement of women and the establishment of gender focal points;

---

[50] *Report of the Fourth World Conference on Women* …

[51] General Assembly resolution 34/180, annex.

[52] *Official Records of the General Assembly, Fifty-second Session, Supplement No. 3* (A/52/3), chap. IV, sect. A, para. 4.

4.   *Acknowledges* that national machineries are necessary for the implementation of the Beijing Platform for Action; and that for national machineries to be effective, clear mandates, location at the highest possible level, accountability mechanisms, partnership with civil society, a transparent political process, adequate financial and human resources and continued strong political commitment are crucial;

5.   *Stresses* the importance of international cooperation in order to assist the work of national mechanisms in all countries, especially developing countries;

6.   *Welcomes* Economic and Social Council decision 1998/298 of 5 August 1998, by which the Council decided to devote the high-level segment of its 1999 substantive session to the advancement of women;

7.   *Proposes*, in order to accelerate the implementation of the strategic objectives of chapter IV.H of the Beijing Platform for Action, that the following action be taken:

Actions by Governments, national machineries and other institutional mechanisms, and the international community, including the United Nations system, for the advancement of women and for gender equality

1.   *Actions to be taken by Governments*

   (*a*)   Provide continued strong political commitment to supporting the strengthening of national machineries and the advancement of women;

   (*b*)   Ensure that national machineries are placed at the highest possible level of government and all institutional mechanisms for the advancement of women are invested with the authority needed to fulfil their mandated roles and responsibilities;

   (*c*)   Provide adequate and sustainable financial and human resources to national machineries and other institutional mechanisms for the advancement of women through national budgets, while also granting national machinery the possibility of attracting funds from other bodies for the purpose of specific projects;

   (*d*)   Structure appropriately the functions of national machineries at all levels in order to ensure effectiveness in gender mainstreaming;

   (*e*)   Ensure that mainstreaming a gender perspective is fully understood, institutionalized and implemented. These efforts should include promoting awareness and understanding of the Platform for Action;

   (*f*)   Continue to take steps to ensure that the integration of a gender perspective in the mainstream of all government activities is part of a dual and complementary strategy to achieve gender equality.

This includes a continuing need for targeted priorities, policies, programmes and positive action measures;

(*g*) Ensure that senior management in each ministry or agency takes responsibility for fulfilling gender equality commitments and integrating a gender perspective in all activities, and that appropriate assistance from gender experts or gender focal points is available;

(*h*) Promote and ensure, as appropriate, the establishment of effective gender focal points at all decision-making levels and in all ministries and other decision-making bodies, develop close collaboration among them and create follow-up mechanisms;

(*i*) Create and/or encourage the creation and strengthening of institutional mechanisms at all levels, including taking all measures to ensure that national machineries as well as focal points within specific institutions are not marginalized in the administrative structure but supported at the highest possible level of government and entrusted with clearly defined mandates which define their function as a policy advisory body;

(*j*) Promote capacity-building including gender training for both women and men in government ministries so as to be more responsive to the needs and interests of women and gender equality, and develop their own capacity by making use of available national and international models and methodologies in the field of gender equality;

(*k*) Promote, where appropriate, and ensure accountability and transparency of government through effective monitoring mechanisms and tools such as gender-disaggregated statistics, gender budgeting, gender auditing and gender impact assessment, based on established benchmarks, and other performance indicators and regular public reporting, including under international agreements;

(*l*) Provide assistance, as appropriate, to agencies including those outside government in formulating gender-sensitive performance indicators, necessary to measure and review progress made in the field of gender equality, including the advancement of women and gender mainstreaming;

(*m*) Continuously improve the gathering and disaggregation of data and the development of statistics and indicators in all critical areas of the Platform for Action for use in analysis, policy development and planning;

(*n*) Give visibility to the relationship between remunerated and unremunerated work and its importance to gender analysis, and promote greater understanding among relevant ministries and organizations by developing methods for assessing its value in quantitative terms in order to develop appropriate policies in this respect;

(*o*) Recognize and acknowledge that unremunerated work by women in, for example, agriculture, food production, natural resources management, caring for dependants and household and voluntary work is a considerable contribution to society. Develop and improve mechanisms, for example time-use studies, to measure in quantitative terms unremunerated work in order to:

- Make visible the unequal distribution between women and men of remunerated and unremunerated work in order to promote changes;

- Assess the real value of unremunerated work and accurately reflect it in satellite or other official accounts that are separate from but consistent with core national accounts;

(*p*) Strengthen the relations among civil society, all governmental agencies and national machineries;

(*q*) Ensure that the needs, rights and interests of all women, including those who are not members of organizations and who live in poverty in rural and urban areas, are identified and mainstreamed into policy and programme development. This should be done in ways that value the diversity of women and recognize the barriers many women face that prohibit and prevent their participation in public policy development;

(*r*) Respect the involvement of non-governmental organizations in assisting Governments in the implementation of regional, national and international commitments through advocacy and raising awareness of gender equality issues. Women should be actively involved in the implementation and monitoring of the Platform for Action;

(*s*) Coordinate or consult with, as appropriate, non-governmental organizations and civil society in national and international activities, including elaborating national action plans, preparing reports to the Committee on the Elimination of Discrimination against Women and implementing the Platform for Action;

(*t*) Ensure transparency through open and participatory dialogue and the promotion of balanced participation of women and men in all areas of decision-making;

(*u*) Support autonomous organizations and institutions involved in research, analysis and evaluation of activities on gender issues and use the results to influence the transformation of policies and programmes;

(*v*) Create clear anti-discrimination regulations with adequate mechanisms, including a proper legal framework for addressing violations;

(*w*) Initiate, where necessary, gender equality legislation and create or strengthen, where appropriate, independent bodies, such as the ombudsperson and equal opportunity commission, with responsibility and authority for, inter alia, promoting and ensuring compliance with gender equality legislation;

(*x*) Involve parliaments and, wherever appropriate, the judiciary in monitoring progress in gender mainstreaming and strengthening gender-related aspects of all government reporting, and ensure transparency through open and participatory dialogue and the promotion of balanced participation of women and men in all areas and at all levels of decision-making.

2. *Actions to be taken by national machineries and other institutional mechanisms*

(*a*) Design, promote the implementation of, execute, monitor, evaluate and mobilize support for policies that promote the advancement of women and advocate gender equality and promote public debate;

(*b*) Act as catalysts for gender mainstreaming in all policies and programmes and not necessarily as agents for policy implementation. However, national machineries are partners in policy formulation and may also choose to implement and coordinate specific projects;

(*c*) Assist other parts of Government in taking specific actions in the gathering and disaggregation of data and the development of statistics and indicators in all critical areas of the Platform for Action for use in analysis, policy development, planning and programming;

(*d*) Promote research and dissemination of research findings and information on women and gender equality, including disparities of income and workload between women and men and, where appropriate, among women;

(*e*) Take specific actions, inter alia, the establishment of documentation centres, to disseminate gender-relevant data and other information, including on the important contribution of women to society and research results in easily accessible formats and places in order to promote more informed public dialogue, including through the media, on gender equality and issues pertinent to the advancement of women;

(*f*) Ensure the ongoing training on gender issues, at all levels, of the personnel of the national machineries to promote programme and policy sustainability;

(*g*) Develop, as appropriate, policies to recruit technical staff with expertise in gender equality issues;

(*h*) Create or strengthen collaborative links with other agencies at local, regional, national and international levels;

(*i*) Recognize civil society as an important source of support and legitimacy and therefore create and strengthen the relationship with civil society through regular consultations with non-governmental organizations, the research community, social partners and other concerned groups. This will create a strong basis for gender-sensitive policy and the advancement of women;

(*j*) Establish partnerships, liaise and consult with women's organizations, non-governmental organizations, academic institutions, the media and other agencies on national and international policies relating to women and gender and inform them of the international commitments of their Governments;

(*k*) Engage the media in dialogue aimed at re-examining gender stereotypes and negative portrayal of both women and men;

(*l*) Create and strengthen collaborative relationships with the private sector, including through initiating advocacy dialogue and advising private companies to address the issues affecting women in the paid labour force, and set up ways and means to promote equality of women and men.

3. *Actions to be taken by the international community, including the United Nations system*

(*a*) Implement Economic and Social Council agreed conclusions 1997/2;

(*b*) Implement fully the revised system-wide medium-term plan for the advancement of women, 1996-2001;

(*c*) Ensure that individual managers are held accountable for implementing the strategic plan of action for the improvement of the status of women in the Secretariat (1995-2000) within their areas of responsibility, and that heads of departments and offices develop gender action plans which establish concrete strategies for the achievement of gender balance in individual departments and offices, with full respect for the principle of equitable geographical distribution and in conformity with Article 101 of the Charter of the United Nations, so as to ensure, as far as possible, that the appointment and promotion of women will not be less than 50 per cent, until the goal of 50/50 gender distribution is met;

(d) Request the Administrative Committee on Coordination Inter-Agency Committee on Women and Gender Equality to continue its work to implement the Beijing Platform for Action and to promote the integration of a gender perspective in the implementation of and follow-up to major United Nations conferences and summits;

(e) Support the implementation of the Beijing Platform for Action, including through support for the important activities of the United Nations Development Fund for Women and the International Research and Training Institute for the Advancement of Women in the fulfilment of their respective mandates;

(f) Support national Governments in their efforts to strengthen national mechanisms through official development assistance and other appropriate assistance;

(g) Encourage multilateral, bilateral, donor and development agencies to include in their programmes of assistance activities that strengthen national machineries;

(h) Encourage Governments and national machineries to undertake wide consultations with their civil societies when providing information on gender and women's issues to relevant international bodies;

(i) Document and publish "good practices", and provide logistical support and ensure equal access to information technology wherever appropriate. In this regard, the offices of United Nations resident coordinators, in particular the women in development programmes and gender units, should play a critical role;

(j) Develop and disseminate gender-disaggregated data and qualitative performance indicators to ensure effective gender-sensitive planning, monitoring, evaluation and implementation of programmes;

(k) Encourage multilateral development institutions, bilateral donors and international non-governmental organizations to make available methodology already developed on the collection and analysis of gender-disaggregated data measurement and valuation of unwaged work and to provide technical assistance and other resources, including financial resources as appropriate, to developing countries and countries with economies in transition;

(l) In order to elaborate a systematic and comprehensive approach to information on unremunerated work, the Division for the

Advancement of Women of the Department of Economic and Social Affairs of the Secretariat should prepare and circulate among all States a detailed and well-structured questionnaire. The questionnaire should seek inputs on developments in measuring and valuing unremunerated work and on policies and programmes as well as laws that recognize and address such work;

(*m*) Request the Division for the Advancement of Women to expand the Directory of National Machineries, by including, for example, mandates, number of staff, e-mail addresses, fax numbers and working-level contacts, so that this comprehensive information can facilitate better communication among national machineries around the world.

Forty-fourth session
28 February–2 March 2000

The Commission acted as the ad hoc preparatory comittee for the twenty-third special session of the United Nations General Assembly, entitled "*Women 2000: Gender equality, development and peace for the twenty-first century*".

No agreed conclusions were adopted.

At the twenty-third special session, in June 2000, the General Assembly adopted by consensus a Political Declaration (General Assembly resolution S-23/2) and "Further actions and initiatives to implement the Beijing Declaration and Platform for Action" (General Assembly resolution S-23/3). The outcome document identified achievements, obstacles and challenges in the implementation of the 12 critical areas of the Platform for Action; and actions and initiatives to overcome obstacles and to achieve the full and accelerated implementation of the Beijing Declaration and Platform for Action.

Forty-fifth session
6-16 March and 9-11 May 2001

Agreed conclusions:

2001/5A. **Women, the girl child and human immuno-deficiency virus/acquired immunodeficiency syndrome**

2001/5B. **Gender and all forms of discrimination, in particular racism, racial discrimination, xenophobia and related intolerance**

The agreed conclusions adopted for the forty-fifth session of the Commission on the Status of Women can be found in the *Resolutions and decisions adopted by the Economic and Social Council at its substantive session of 2001* (E/2001/INF/2/Add.2), resolution 2001/5.

Agreed conclusions 2001/5A

Women, the girl child and human immunodeficiency virus/acquired immunodeficiency syndrome

1. Women play a vital role in the social and economic development of their countries. It is a profound concern that by the end of 2000, 36.1 million people were living with HIV/AIDS, and of those infected, 95 per cent were living in developing countries, and 16.4 million were women. The proportion of women infected with HIV is increasing and in sub-Saharan Africa women constitute 55 per cent of all adult HIV-infected, while teenage girls are infected at a rate of five to six times greater than their male counterparts.

2. Full enjoyment by women and girls of all human rights, civil, cultural, economic, political and social, including the right to development— which are universal, indivisible, interdependent and interrelated—is of crucial importance in preventing further spread of HIV/AIDS. The majority of women and girls do not fully enjoy their rights, in particular to education, the highest attainable standard of physical and mental health and social security, especially in developing countries. These inequalities begin early in life and render women and girls more vulnerable in the area of sexual and reproductive health, thus increasing their risk and vulnerability to HIV infection and their disproportionate suffering from the consequences of the HIV/AIDS epidemic.

3. Poverty, negative and harmful traditional and customary practices that subordinate women in the household, community and society render women especially vulnerable to HIV/sexually transmitted infections. Millions of women and girls lack access and/or have insufficient access to health care, medication and social support in general, including in the case of sexually transmitted infections/HIV/AIDS.

4. The Commission on the Status of Women has taken into account the recommendations on women, the girl child and HIV/AIDS as contained in the following documents: the Beijing Platform for Action,[53] the Programme of Action of the International Conference on Population and Development,[54] the Copenhagen Programme of Action,[55] the outcome doc-

---

[53] *Report of the Fourth World Conference on Women ...*

[54] See *Report of the International Conference on Population and Development, Cairo, 5-13 September 1994* (United Nations publication, Sales No. E.95.XIII.18), chap. I, resolution I, annex.

[55] *Report of the World Summit for Social Development, Copenhagen, 6-12 March 1995* (United Nations publication, Sales No. E.96.IV.8), chap. I, resolution I, annex II.

uments of the twenty-first, twenty-third and twenty-fourth special sessions of the General Assembly,[56] the United Nations Millennium Declaration,[57] the agreed conclusions of the Commission on the Status of Women on women and health,[58] and Commission resolution 44/2.[59]

5.   The Commission recalls the internationally agreed targets as contained in the documents referred to in paragraph 4 above, and suggests that the outcome document of the special session of the General Assembly on HIV/AIDS should fully integrate a gender perspective, including in any new targets, and focus on actions needed to achieve existing targets.

6.   The Commission welcomes the Abuja Declaration on HIV/AIDS, Tuberculosis and other Related Infectious Diseases, in particular its gender dimension, adopted by the Organization of African Unity at its Special Summit on HIV/AIDS, held at Abuja, Nigeria, in April 2001.

7.   The Commission notes with appreciation the efforts of the Joint United Nations Programme on HIV/AIDS and its co-sponsors, bilateral and multilateral donors, governmental, intergovernmental and non-governmental organizations in their efforts to empower women through capacity development programmes, as well as programmes that provide women with access to development resources and strengthen their networks that offer care and support to women affected by HIV/AIDS.

8.   The highest level of political commitment to the empowerment and advancement of women and to the prevention, research, care and treatment of sexually transmitted infections, especially HIV/AIDS, must be secured.

9.   It is important to fully integrate a gender perspective in the preparatory process and in the outcome document of the special session of the General Assembly on HIV/AIDS, including, inter alia, the full integration of a gender perspective in any new targets and in actions needed to achieve internationally agreed targets that relate to women, the girl child and HIV/AIDS as contained in the documents referred to in paragraph 4 above.

10.   In order to accelerate the implementation of the strategic objectives of the conferences and documents mentioned in paragraph 4 above, especially of those objectives related to women, the girl child and HIV/AIDS, the Commission recommends that the following actions be taken:

---

[56]   See General Assembly resolutions S-21/2, annex, S-23/2, annex, S-23/3, annex, and S-24/2, annex.

[57]   General Assembly resolution 55/2.

[58]   See Economic and Social Council resolution 1999/17, sect. I.

[59]   See *Official Records of the Economic and Social Council, 2000, Supplement No. 7* (E/2000/27), chap. I, sect. C.

Actions to be taken by Governments, the United Nations system and civil society, as appropriate

1. *Empowerment of women*

    (a) The rapid progression of the HIV/AIDS pandemic, particularly in the developing world, has had a devastating impact on women. The unequal power relationships between women and men, in which women often do not have the power to insist on safe and responsible sex practices, and lack of communication and understanding between women and men on women's health needs, inter alia, endanger women's health, particularly by increasing their susceptibility to sexually transmitted infections, including HIV/AIDS;

    (b) Responsible behaviour and gender equality are among the important prerequisites for its prevention;

    (c) Ensure that the sexual health and reproductive rights of women of all ages as defined in paragraphs 94, 95 and 96 of the Beijing Platform for Action are seen as an essential part in efforts to promote women's empowerment, bearing in mind that women and girls are disproportionately affected by HIV/AIDS, and, in this context, further promote the advancement and empowerment of women and women's full enjoyment of all human rights, including the right to development and their right to have control over and decide freely and responsibly on matters related to their sexuality, in order to protect themselves from high risk and irresponsible behaviour leading to sexually transmitted infections, including HIV/AIDS, and access to health information and education, health care and health services, which are critical to increasing the ability of women and young girls to protect themselves from HIV infection;

    (d) Focus national and international policies towards the eradication of poverty in order to empower women to better protect themselves from the spread of the pandemic and to deal more effectively with the adverse effects of HIV/AIDS;

    (e) Alleviate the social and economic impact of HIV/AIDS on women who in their roles as food suppliers and traditional caregivers are primarily affected by the negative consequences of the pandemic, such as a reduced labour force and a breakdown of social service systems;

    (f) Reaffirm the equal rights of women and the girl child infected and affected by sexually transmitted infections/HIV/AIDS to have access to health, education and social services and to be protected from all forms of discrimination, stigma, abuse and neglect;

(*g*) Also reaffirm the human rights of girls and women to equal access to education, skill training and employment opportunities as a means to reduce their vulnerability to sexually transmitted diseases/HIV;

(*h*) Urge Governments to take all necessary measures to empower women and strengthen women's economic independence and protect and promote full enjoyment of all human rights and fundamental freedoms in order to allow women and girls to better protect themselves from sexually transmitted infections/HIV;

(*i*) Address and reduce the increased HIV/AIDS risks, vulnerabilities and impact on women and girls, including in conflict situations, through gender-sensitive economic, legal and social services and programmes, including integration of HIV/AIDS prevention and care services into minimum essential health-care packages;

(*j*) Strengthen concrete measures to eliminate all forms of violence against women and girls, including harmful traditional and customary practices, abuse and rape, battering and trafficking in women and girls, which aggravate the conditions fostering the spread of HIV/AIDS, through, inter alia, the enactment and enforcement of laws, as well as public campaigns to combat violence against women and girls;

(*k*) Take steps to create an environment that promotes all human rights, compassion and support for people infected/affected by HIV/AIDS, including through introducing and/or reviewing legislation with a view to striving to remove discriminatory provisions, and provide the legal framework that will protect the rights of people living with HIV/AIDS, particularly of women and girls, and enable those who are vulnerable to have access to appropriate voluntary and confidential counselling services, and encourage efforts to reduce discrimination and stigmatization;

(*l*) Further develop and fully integrate a gender perspective into national, regional and international HIV/AIDS programmes and strategies, taking into account, inter alia, sex- and age-disaggregated data and statistics, with a particular focus on gender equality;

(*m*) Take measures to promote and implement women's equal access to and control over economic resources, including land, property rights and the right to inheritance, regardless of their marital status, in order to reduce the vulnerability of women in the context of the HIV/AIDS epidemic;

(*n*) Provide women and girls, including those in marginalized groups, with equal access to quality education, literacy programmes, health care and health services, social services, skills training and employment opportunities, support capacity-building and the strengthening of women's networks and protect them from all forms of discrimination, including racial discrimination, stigma, abuse and neglect, in order to reduce their risk and vulnerability to HIV/AIDS and alleviate the impact on those infected and affected by HIV/AIDS.

2. *Prevention*

(*a*) Governments, relevant United Nations agencies, funds and programmes and intergovernmental and non-governmental organizations, individually and collectively, should make efforts to place combating HIV/AIDS as a priority on the development agenda and to implement multisectoral and decentralized effective preventive strategies and programmes, especially for the most vulnerable populations, including women, young girls and infants, also taking into account the prevention of mother-to-child transmission;

(*b*) Governments, with the assistance of relevant United Nations agencies, funds and programmes, must adopt a long-term, timely, coherent and integrated AIDS prevention policy, with public information, life skills–based education programmes specifically tailored to the needs of women and girls adapted to their social and cultural context and sensitivities and the specific needs in their life cycle;

(*c*) Intensify efforts to determine the best policies and programmes to prevent women and young girls from becoming infected with HIV/AIDS, taking into account that women, in particular young girls, are socially, physiologically and biologically more vulnerable than men to sexually transmitted infections;

(*d*) Take measures to integrate, inter alia, a family-based approach in programmes aiming at providing prevention, care and support to women and girls infected and affected by HIV/AIDS, and take measures to integrate a community-based approach in policies and programmes aimed at providing prevention, care and support to women and girls infected and affected by HIV/AIDS;

(*e*) Ensure equal and non-discriminatory access to accurate, comprehensive information, to prevention education on reproductive health, and to voluntary testing and counselling services and technologies within a cultural and gender-sensitive framework and with particular emphasis on adolescents and young adults;

(*f*) Request the Joint United Nations Programme on HIV/AIDS and its co-sponsors to continue in their efforts aimed at providing complete and accurate sexual and reproductive health education for young people, within a cultural and gender-sensitive framework, while, inter alia, encouraging them to delay sexual initiation, and/or to use condoms, and, in this context, urge that greater attention be given to the education of men and boys about their roles and their responsibilities in preventing the transmission of sexually transmitted diseases, including HIV/AIDS, to their partners;

(g) Promote gender equality in relationships, and provide information and resources to promote informed, responsible and safe sexual behaviour and practices, mutual respect and gender equality in sexual relationships;

(h) Encourage all forms of media to promote non-discriminatory and gender-sensitive images and a culture of non-violence and respect for all human rights, particularly women's rights, in addressing HIV/AIDS;

(i) Encourage active involvement of men and boys through, inter alia, youth-led and youth-specific HIV education projects and peer-based programmes, in challenging gender stereotypes and attitudes as well as gender inequalities in relation to HIV and AIDS, as well as their full participation in prevention, impact alleviation and care, and design and implement programmes to encourage and enable men to adopt safe and responsible sexual and reproductive behaviour and to use effectively methods to prevent unwanted pregnancies and sexually transmitted infections, including HIV/AIDS;

(j) Intensify, especially in the most affected countries, education, services, community-based mobilization and information strategies to protect women of all ages from HIV and other sexually transmitted infections, including through the development of safe, affordable, effective and easily accessible female-controlled methods, including such methods as microbicides and female condoms that protect against sexually transmitted infections and HIV/AIDS, as well as voluntary and confidential HIV testing and counselling and the promotion of sexually responsible behaviour, including abstinence and condom use;

(k) Strengthen sustainable, efficient and accessible primary health-care systems that serve to support prevention efforts;

(l) Special attention should be given to the prevention of HIV, particularly with regard to mother-to-child transmission and for victims of rape—on the basis of informed consent and voluntary and confidential testing, counselling and treatment—including through ensuring access to care and improving the quality and availability of affordable drugs and diagnostics, especially anti-retroviral therapies, and by building on existing efforts, with special attention to the issue of breastfeeding;

(*m*) Strive to ensure that schools at all levels, other educational institutions and non-formal systems of education play a leading role in preventing HIV infection, preventing and combating stigmatization and discrimination through the provision of an environment free of all forms of violence that promotes compassion and tolerance, and provide gender-sensitive education, including on responsible sexual behaviour, and practices, life skills and behaviour change;

(*n*) Work together with civil society, including traditional, community and religious leaders, to identify the customary and traditional practices that adversely influence gender relations, and to eliminate those practices that increase the vulnerability of women and girls to HIV/AIDS.

3. *Treatment, care and support*

(*a*) Request Governments to ensure universal and equal access for women and men throughout their life cycle to social services related to health care, including education, clean water and safe sanitation, nutrition, food security and health education programmes, especially for women and girls living with and affected by HIV/AIDS, including treatment for opportunistic diseases;

(*b*) Request Governments to work to provide comprehensive health care for women and girls living with HIV/AIDS, including dietary and food supplements and treatment for opportunistic infections and full, equal, non-discriminatory and prompt access to health care and health services, including sexual and reproductive health and voluntary and confidential counselling, taking into account the rights of the child to access to information, privacy, confidentiality, respect and informed consent and the responsibilities, rights and duties of parents and legal guardians;

(*c*) Care and support for people living with HIV/AIDS, particularly women and girls, should have a comprehensive approach, involving medical, social, psychological, spiritual and economic needs, targeting the community and national levels;

(*d*) Collaborate to strengthen efforts to create an environment and the conditions necessary, with the assistance of relevant United Nations agencies, funds and programmes and intergovernmental and non-governmental organizations, upon request, to address the challenges faced by women and girls infected and affected by HIV/AIDS, particularly orphans and widows, girls and older women who may also be primary caregivers for people living with HIV/AIDS, all of whom are particularly vulnerable to both economic and sexual exploitation; provide them with the necessary economic and psychosocial support; and encourage their economic independence through income-generating programmes and other methods;

(e) Provide support for the implementation of special programmes for the growing problems of children orphaned by AIDS, especially girls, who may easily become victims of sexual exploitation.

4. *Enabling environment for regional and international cooperation*

(a) Call upon the international community, relevant agencies, funds and programmes of the United Nations system and intergovernmental and non-governmental organizations to intensify their support of national efforts against HIV/AIDS, particularly in favour of women and young girls, including efforts to provide affordable antiretroviral drugs, diagnostics and drugs to treat tuberculosis and other opportunistic infections; strengthening health systems, including reliable distribution and delivery systems; implementing a strong generic drug policy; bulk purchasing; negotiating with pharmaceutical companies to reduce prices; appropriate financing systems; and encouraging local manufacturing and import practices consistent with national laws and international agreements, particularly in the worst-hit regions in Africa and where the epidemic is severely setting back national development gains;

(b) Take action to eradicate poverty, which is a major contributory factor for the spread of HIV infection and worsens the impact of the epidemic, particularly for women and girls, as well as depleting resources and incomes of families and endangering the survival of present and future generations;

(c) Identify and implement development-oriented and durable solutions that integrate a gender perspective to external debt and debt-servicing problems of developing countries, including least developed countries, inter alia, through debt relief, including the option of debt cancellation for official development assistance in order to help them to finance programmes and projects targeted at development, including the advancement of women, inter alia, through facilitating the delivery of health care and health services and the provision of preventive programmes on HIV/AIDS, especially targeting women and girls; in this regard, welcome the Cologne initiative for the reduction of debt, particularly the speedy implementation of the enhanced heavily indebted poor countries initiatives; and encourage Governments to ensure the provision of adequate funds for its implementation and implement the provision that funds saved should be used to support anti-poverty programmes that are gender sensitive and that address prevention, care and support of women and girls infected and affected;

(*d*) Ensure international, regional and South-South cooperation, including development assistance and additional adequate resources to implement gender-sensitive policies and programmes aimed at halting the spread of the epidemic in providing affordable quality treatment and care of all people, especially women and girls living with HIV/AIDS;

(*e*) Encourage the Joint United Nations Programme on HIV/AIDS and its co-sponsors, bilateral and multilateral donors and intergovernmental and non-governmental organizations to intensify their support to empower women and prevent HIV infection and to give urgent and priority attention to the situation of women and girls, especially in Africa, in particular through the International Partnership against AIDS in Africa;

(*f*) Increase investment in research on the development of HIV vaccines, microbicides and other female-controlled methods, simpler and less expensive diagnostic tests, single-dose treatments for sexually transmitted infections and quality low-cost drug combinations, including for opportunistic infections and sexually transmitted infections, as well as alternative medicine for HIV/AIDS, focusing on the needs of women and girls;

(*g*) Support and assist research and development centres, in particular at the national level, in the worst-hit regions with a gender-specific focus, in the field of vaccines and treatment for HIV/AIDS, as well as support the efforts by Governments in building and/or strengthening their national capacities in this area;

(*h*) Develop and implement as well as strengthen already existing training programmes for law enforcement officers, prison officers, medical officers and judicial personnel, as well as United Nations personnel, including peacekeeping staff, to be more sensitive and responsive to the needs of threatened and abused women and children infected with HIV/AIDS, including intravenous drug users, female inmates and orphans;

(*i*) Ensure that the needs of girls and women in relation to HIV/AIDS in all situations of conflict, post-conflict and peacekeeping and in the immediate and reconstructive responses to emergencies and natural disasters are addressed;

(*j*)   Provide gender-sensitive prevention and treatment services for female substance abusers living with HIV/AIDS;

(*k*)   Provide technical and financial support to networks of people living with HIV/AIDS, non-governmental organizations and community-based organizations involved in implementing HIV/AIDS programmes, particularly women's groups, in order to strengthen their efforts;

(*l*)   Adopt a balanced approach to prevention and comprehensive care, including treatment and support, for women and girls affected by HIV/AIDS, taking into account the role played by poverty, poor nutritional conditions and underdevelopment, which increases the vulnerability of women and girls to HIV/AIDS;

(*m*)   Urge relevant United Nations entities to incorporate a gender perspective into their follow-up and evaluation of the progress made on the control of sexually transmitted infections and HIV/AIDS;

(*n*)   Commend UNAIDS for its advocacy in successfully accelerating both increased prevention and improved access to care and urge Governments and the international community to continue advocating, lobbying and encouraging Governments to enter into negotiations with multinational drug companies for reduction in market prices of HIV/AIDS-related drugs and diagnostics to ensure availability, affordability and sustainability to women and girls living with HIV/AIDS.

Agreed conclusions 2001/5B

Gender and all forms of discrimination, in particular racism, racial discrimination, xenophobia and related intolerance

1.   The Charter of the United Nations, the Universal Declaration of Human Rights,[60] the International Convention on the Elimination of All Forms of Racial Discrimination,[61] the Convention on the Elimination of All Forms of Discrimination against Women[62] and other international instruments reaffirm the principles of equality and non-discrimination.

---

[60]   General Assembly resolution 217 A (III).

[61]   General Assembly resolution 2106 A (XX), annex.

[62]   General Assembly resolution 34/180.

2. The consistent efforts of the international community in promoting gender equality through the convening of world conferences on women are recalled. It should also be recalled that the Vienna Declaration and Programme of Action adopted by the World Conference on Human Rights,[63] the Beijing Declaration[64] and Platform for Action adopted at the Fourth World Conference on Women and the outcome documents of the special session of the General Assembly entitled "Women 2000: gender equality, development and peace for the twenty-first century" emphasize that all human rights of women and of the girl child are an inalienable, integral and indivisible part of universal human rights. The Platform for Action reaffirms that all human rights—civil, cultural, economic, political and social, including the right to development—are universal, indivisible, interdependent and interrelated.

3. The Beijing Declaration and Platform for Action indicate that many women face additional barriers to the enjoyment of their human rights because of such factors as their race, language, ethnicity, culture, religion, disability or socio-economic class or because they are indigenous people, migrants, including women migrant workers, displaced women or refugees. Also, the outcome documents of the special session indicate that in situations of armed conflict and foreign occupation, human rights of women have been extensively violated. Among the further actions and initiatives to implement the platform adopted by the special session were several directed at the elimination of racially motivated violence against women and girls.

4. The efforts of the international community in combating racism, racial discrimination, xenophobia and related intolerance are recalled.

5. There has been growing recognition that various types of discrimination do not always affect women and men in the same way. Moreover, gender discrimination may be intensified and facilitated by all other forms of discrimination. It has been increasingly recognized that without gender analysis of all forms of discrimination, including multiple forms of discrimination and, in particular, in this context, racial discrimination, xenophobia and related intolerance, violations of the human rights of women might escape detection and remedies to address racism may also fail to meet the needs of women and girls. It is also important that efforts to address gender discrimination incorporate approaches to the elimination of all forms of discrimination, including racial discrimination.

6. By its resolution 52/111, the General Assembly decided to convene a World Conference against Racism, Racial Discrimination, Xenophobia and Related Intolerance, to be held in Durban from 31 August to 7 September 2001. In its resolution 53/132, the Assembly proclaimed 2001 as the

---

[63]   A/CONF.157/24 (Part I), chap. III.

[64]   *Report of the Fourth World Conference on Women …*

International Year of Mobilization against Racism, Racial Discrimination, Xenophobia and Related Intolerance. It is therefore timely that the gender dimensions of racism, racial discrimination, xenophobia and related intolerance are addressed by the Commission on the Status of Women.

7.   The increasing gravity of different manifestations of racism, racial discrimination and xenophobia in various parts of the world requires a more integrated and effective approach on the part of relevant mechanisms of the United Nations human rights machinery. These trends affect the implementation of the outcome documents of the special session of the General Assembly entitled "Women 2000: gender equality, development and peace for the twenty-first century" and of the relevant international instruments against discrimination.

8.   The Commission recommends that the following actions be taken:

Actions to be taken by Governments, the United Nations and civil society, as appropriate

1.   *An integrated, holistic approach to address multiple forms of discrimination against women and girls, in particular racism, racial discrimination, xenophobia and related intolerance*

　　(*a*)　Examine the intersection of multiple forms of discrimination, including their root causes, from a gender perspective with special emphasis on gender-based racial discrimination in order to develop and implement strategies, policies and programmes aimed at the elimination of all forms of discrimination against women and to increase the role that women play in the design, implementation and monitoring of gender-sensitive anti-racist policies;

　　(*b*)　Establish and strengthen effective partnerships with and provide support, as appropriate, to all relevant actors of civil society, including non-governmental organizations working to promote gender equality and advancement of women, in particular women subject to multiple discrimination, in order to promote an integrated and holistic approach to the elimination of all forms of discrimination against women and girls;

　　(*c*)　Acknowledge the need to address the issues of racism, racial discrimination, xenophobia and related intolerance as and where they affect young women and men, boys and girls and recognize the role they play in the fight against racism, racial discrimination, xenophobia and related intolerance, including particular forms of racism experienced by young women and girls, and support the fundamental role played by youth non-governmental organizations in educating young people and children to build a society based on respect and solidarity;

(*d*) Promote respect for and value of the full diversity of women's and girls' situations and conditions, recognizing that some women face particular barriers to their empowerment; ensure that the goals of achieving gender equality and advancement of women, including marginalized women, are reflected in all strategies, policies and programmes aimed at the elimination of all forms of discrimination against women and girls; and mainstream a gender perspective into the preparation and implementation of policies integrating multiculturalism, ensuring the full enjoyment of all human rights and fundamental freedoms by all women and girls and reaffirming that human rights—civil, cultural, economical, political and social, including the right to development—are universal, indivisible, interdependent and interrelated;

(*e*) Promote recognition that the empowerment of women is an essential component of a proactive strategy to fight racism, racial discrimination, xenophobia and other forms of related intolerance and take measures to empower women subject to multiple discrimination to exercise their rights fully in all spheres of life and to play an active role in the design and implementation of policies and measures that affect their lives;

(*f*) Take action to raise awareness and promote the eradication of all forms of discrimination, including multiple discrimination experienced by women, through, inter alia, education and mass media campaigns;

(*g*) The Platform for Action recognized that women face barriers to full equality and advancement because of such factors as their race, age, language, ethnicity, culture, religion or disability, because they are indigenous women or of other status. Many women encounter specific obstacles related to their family status, particularly as single parents, and their socio-economic status, including their living conditions in rural, isolated or impoverished areas. Additional barriers also exist for refugee women, other displaced women, including internally displaced women, and for immigrant women and migrant women, including women migrant workers. Many women are also particularly affected by environmental disasters, serious and infectious diseases and various forms of violence against women;

(*h*) Acknowledge that racism, racial discrimination, xenophobia and related intolerance manifest themselves in a differentiated manner for women, increasing poverty, causing their living conditions to deteriorate, generating violence and limiting or denying them the full enjoyment and exercise of all their human rights;

(*i*) Ensure the full and equal opportunity for the sustained partici- pation and representation of indigenous women and girls and women and girls, as appropriate, from culturally diverse back- grounds in all relevant decision-making processes;

(*j*) Ensure that the Commission on the Status of Women takes into account in its work the impact of all forms of discrimination, including multiple discrimination on women's advancement;

(*k*) Acknowledge the ongoing work of the Committee on the Elimina- tion of Discrimination against Women and the Committee on the Elimination of Racial Discrimination in taking into account the impact of multiple forms of discrimination on women's advance- ment and the achievement of gender equality.

2. *Policies, legal measures, mechanisms and machineries*

(*a*) Establish and/or strengthen, where appropriate, legislation and regulations against all forms of racism, racial discrimination, xenophobia and related intolerance, including their gender-based manifestations;

(*b*) Condemn all forms of racism and racial discrimination, includ- ing propaganda, activities and organizations based on doctrines of superiority of one race or group of persons that attempt to jus- tify or promote racism or racial discrimination in any form;

(*c*) Take concrete measures to promote equality based on the elimi- nation of gender and racial prejudice in all fields, through, inter alia, improving access to education, health care, employment and other basic services to promote full enjoyment of economic, social and cultural rights for all women and girls;

(*d*) Take measures to address, through policies and programmes, rac- ism and racially motivated violence against women and girls and to increase cooperation, policy responses, effective implementa- tion of national legislation and other protective and preventive measures aimed at the elimination of all forms of violence against women and girls;

(*e*) Review, where appropriate, national legal and other mechanisms, including the criminal justice system, to ensure equality before the law so that women and girls can seek protection, shelter and remedies against all forms of discrimination, including intersec- tional discrimination;

(*f*) Review, where appropriate, policies and laws, including those on citizenship, immigration and asylum, for their impact on the elimination of all forms of discrimination against women and the achievement of gender equality;

(*g*) Design and implement policies and measures that address all forms of violence against women and girls, and empower victims of all forms of violence, in particular women and girls, to regain control over their lives, inter alia, through special protection and assistance measures;

(*h*) Devise, enforce and strengthen effective measures to combat and eliminate all forms of trafficking in women and girls through a comprehensive anti-trafficking strategy consisting of, inter alia, legislative measures, prevention campaigns, information exchange, assistance and protection for and reintegration of the victims and prosecution of all the offenders involved, including intermediaries;

(*i*) Develop and implement policies to ensure the full enjoyment of all human rights and fundamental freedoms by all women and girls regardless of race, colour, descent or national or ethnic origin;

(*j*) Take measures, as appropriate, to promote and strengthen policies and programmes for indigenous women with their full participation and respect for their cultural diversity, to combat discrimination based on gender and race and to ensure their full enjoyment of all human rights;

(*k*) Review and revise, as appropriate, emigration policies with a view to eliminating all discriminatory policies and practices against migrants, especially women and children, and to protect fully all their human rights, regardless of their legal status, as well as to provide them with humane treatment;

(*l*) Take steps to eliminate any violations of the human rights of women refugees, asylum-seekers and internally displaced persons who are often subjected to sexual and other violence;

(*m*) Urge all States that have not yet done so to become parties to the International Convention on the Elimination of All Forms of Racial Discrimination in order to achieve its universal ratification and emphasize the importance of the full compliance of States parties with the obligations they have accepted under this Convention;

(*n*) Consider signing, ratifying or acceding to the International Convention on the Protection of the Rights of All Migrant Workers and Members of Their Families[65] as a matter of priority, and consider promoting ratification of the relevant conventions of the International Labour Organization.

---

[65] General Assembly resolution 45/158.

3.   *Change attitudes and eliminate stereotypes and prejudice*

(a)   Develop gender-sensitive education and training programmes aimed at eliminating discriminatory attitudes towards women and girls, and adopt measures to address the intersection between racist and gender-based stereotypes;

(b)   Develop and implement programmes and policies to raise awareness among all relevant actors at national, regional and international levels to the issue of multiple discrimination against women and girls;

(c)   Review and update educational materials, including textbooks, and take appropriate action to remove all elements promoting discrimination, in particular gender-based discrimination, racism, racial discrimination, xenophobia and related intolerance;

(d)   Ensure that education and training, especially teacher training, promote respect for human rights, the culture of peace, gender equality and cultural, religious and other diversity, and encourage educational and training institutions and organizations to adopt policies of equal opportunities and follow up their implementation with the participation of teachers, parents, boys and girls and the community;

(e)   Develop strategies to increase awareness among men and boys with respect to their shared responsibility in promoting gender equality and combating all forms of discrimination, in particular racism, racial discrimination, xenophobia and related intolerance as well as multiple discrimination;

(f)   Develop anti-racist and gender-sensitive human rights training for personnel in the administration of justice, law enforcement agencies, security and health-care, services, schools and migration authorities, paying particular attention to immigration officials, border police and staff of migrant detention centres, as well as for United Nations personnel;

(g)   Bearing in mind the gender perspective, encourage the mass media to promote ideas of tolerance and understanding among peoples and different cultures.

4.   *Research and collection of data and information*

(a)   Develop methodologies to identify the ways in which various forms of discrimination converge and affect women and girls and conduct studies on how racism, racial discrimination, xenophobia and related intolerance are reflected in laws, policies, institutions and practices and how this has contributed to the vulnerability, victimization, marginalization and exclusion of women and the girl child;

(*b*) Collect, analyse and disseminate quantitative, qualitative and gender-sensitive data regarding the impact of all forms of discrimination, including multiple discrimination, on women and girls and sponsor, where appropriate, surveys and community-based research, including the collection of disaggregated data by sex, age and other variables, as appropriate.

5. *Preventing conflict and promoting a culture of peace, equality, non-discrimination, respect and tolerance*

(*a*) Respect fully international human rights law and international humanitarian law applicable to the rights and protection of women and girls and take special measures to protect women and girls from gender-based violence, particularly rape and all other forms of sexual violence during armed conflict, and end impunity and prosecute those responsible for genocide, crimes against humanity and war crimes, including those relating to sexual and other gender-based violence against women and girls;

(*b*) Violence against women and girls is a major obstacle to the achievement of the objectives of gender equality, development and peace. Violence against women both violates and impairs or nullifies the enjoyment by women of their human rights and fundamental freedoms. Gender-based violence, such as battering and other domestic violence, sexual abuse, sexual slavery and exploitation, international trafficking in women and children, forced prostitution and sexual harassment, as well as violence against women resulting from cultural prejudice, racism and racial discrimination, xenophobia, pornography, ethnic cleansing, armed conflict, foreign occupation, religious and anti-religious extremism and terrorism, are incompatible with the dignity and worth of the human person and must be combated and eliminated;

(*c*) Ensure the full and equal opportunity for sustained participation and representation of women at all levels and in all areas in conflict prevention, management and conflict resolution and in post-conflict peacebuilding.

6. *World Conference against Racism, Racial Discrimination, Xenophobia and Related Intolerance*

The Commission on the Status of Women stresses the importance of mainstreaming a gender perspective into the preparations, work and outcome of the World Conference, and urges the inclusion of women in delegations to the Conference.

Forty-sixth session
4-15 and 25 March 2002

Agreed conclusions:

2002/5A.   **Eradicating poverty, including through the empowerment of women throughout their life cycle, in a globalizing world**

2002/5B.   **Environmental management and the mitigation of natural disasters**

The agreed conclusions adopted for the forty-sixth session of the Commission on the Status of Women can be found in the *Resolutions and decisions adopted by the Economic and Social Council at its substantive session of 2002* (E/2002/INF/2/Add.2), resolution 2002/5.

Agreed conclusions 2002/5A

Eradicating poverty, including through the empowerment of women throughout their life cycle, in a globalizing world

1. The Commission on the Status of Women recalls and reiterates the strategic objectives and actions of the Beijing Platform for Action[66] and the outcome document adopted at the twenty-third special session of the General Assembly entitled "Women 2000: gender equality, development and peace for the twenty-first century",[67] which emphasized the multidimensional nature of poverty and identified gender equality and the empowerment of women as critical factors in the eradication of poverty. It also recalls the United Nations Millennium Declaration[68] and the development goals contained therein, as well as the resolve to promote gender equality and the empowerment of women as effective ways to combat poverty, hunger and disease and to stimulate development that is truly sustainable.

2. The Commission on the Status of Women recognizes that, while it is the primary responsibility of States to attain economic and social development and to achieve the development and poverty eradication goals as set out in the United Nations Millennium Declaration, the international community should support the efforts of the developing countries to eradicate poverty and ensure basic social protection and to promote an enabling international environment.

3. While globalization has brought greater economic opportunities and autonomy to some women, many others, owing to the deepening inequalities among and within countries, have been marginalized and deprived of the benefits of this process. Globalization should be fully inclusive and equitable. To that end, there is a strong need for policies and measures at the national and international levels, formulated and implemented with the full and effective participation of developing countries and countries with economies in transition to help them to respond effectively to those challenges and opportunities. Further efforts at the national and international levels should be made to eliminate the obstacles facing the integration of developing countries in the global economy.

4. The empowerment of women is the process by which women take control over their lives, acquiring the ability to make strategic choices. Empowerment is an important strategy to eradicate poverty. Special atten-

---

[66] *Report of the Fourth World Conference on Women ...*

[67] General Assembly resolution S-23/3, annex.

[68] See General Assembly resolution 55/2.

tion must be given to the situation of women and children, who often bear the greatest burden of extreme poverty.

5. The Commission urges Governments and, as appropriate, the relevant funds and programmes, organizations and the specialized agencies of the United Nations system, the international financial institutions, civil society, including the private sector and non-governmental organizations (NGOs), and other stakeholders to take the following actions to accelerate implementation of these strategic objectives to address the needs of all women:

(*a*) Ensure that all actions to achieve the poverty eradication goals established in the United Nations Millennium Declaration include the promotion of gender equality and the empowerment of women throughout their life cycle;

(*b*) Ensure that, in order to eradicate poverty and promote gender equality and democracy and strengthen the rule of law, both women and men are involved in decision-making, political agenda-setting and allocation of resources;

(*c*) Ensure that women and men have equal access to full and effective participation in all processes and that a gender perspective is mainstreamed in development, trade and financial institutions;

(*d*) Create an enabling environment and design and implement policies that promote and protect the enjoyment of all human rights—civil, cultural, economic, political and social rights, including the right to development—and fundamental freedoms, as part of the efforts to achieve gender equality, development and peace;

(*e*) Evaluate the relationship between the empowerment of women and poverty eradication in different stages of women's life cycle and analyse the intersection of gender and other factors, reflect the implications for policies and programmes and compile and widely disseminate good practices and lessons learned;

(*f*) Strengthen efforts to mainstream gender perspectives and the empowerment of women through the whole policy process, from the identification to the formulation, implementation, evaluation and follow-up of macroeconomic policies, as well as economic and social policy formulation and implementation and poverty eradication policies, programmes, development frameworks and strategies;

(*g*) Establish or improve gender-specific analysis of poverty and strengthen institutional capacities at all levels, including relevant national machineries, in order to undertake gender analysis in poverty eradication initiatives by, inter alia, the allocation of sufficient resources;

(*h*) Improve the collection, compilation and dissemination of timely, reliable, comparable data disaggregated by sex and age and further develop quantitative and qualitative indicators, including social indicators, by national and international statistical organizations so as to increase capacity to measure, assess and analyse poverty among women and men, including at the household level, and make progress in the empowerment of women throughout their life cycle;

(*i*) Encourage the inclusion of data on women's equal access to land and other property in United Nations reports;

(*j*) Identify and take all appropriate measures to address obstacles to the empowerment of women and to their full enjoyment of all human rights and fundamental freedoms throughout the life cycle with a view to eradicating poverty;

(*k*) Take the strongest measures to eliminate all forms of discrimination and violence against women and girls;

(*l*) Incorporate a gender perspective into the design, development, adoption and execution of all budgetary processes, as well as economic and financial policies, in a transparent manner so as to ensure, where appropriate, that national budget policies and priorities as well as resource allocations support the eradication of poverty, the empowerment of women and the achievement of gender equality goals, and ensure full participation by women in all such processes;

(*m*) Review and reform, where appropriate, fiscal policies, particularly taxation policies, to ensure equality between women and men in this regard;

(*n*) Strengthen the provision of and ensure access to adequate, affordable and accessible public and social services to meet the needs of all women, in particular women living in poverty;

(*o*) Design, implement and promote family-friendly policies and services, including affordable, accessible and quality care services for children and other dependants, parental and other leave schemes and campaigns to sensitize public opinion and other relevant actors on equal sharing of employment and family responsibilities between women and men;

(*p*) Improve and develop physical and mental health programmes and services, including preventive health care, for women, particularly women living in poverty;

(*q*) Strengthen policies and programmes at the national level to provide equal access to health-care services for all women and girls, particularly for those living in poverty;

(r) Create and ensure equal access to all types of permanent and sustainable social protection/social security systems at all stages throughout women's life cycle, taking into account the specific needs of all women living in poverty;

(s) Ensure full and equal access at all levels to formal and non-formal education and training for women and girls, including pregnant adolescents and adolescent mothers, as key to their empowerment by, inter alia, the reallocation of resources, as necessary;

(t) Take urgent and effective measures in accordance with international law with a view to alleviating the negative impact of economic sanctions on women and children;

(u) Enhance market access for developing countries and countries with economies in transition, in particular for those sectors that provide greater employment opportunities for women, and expand access for women entrepreneurs to trade opportunities;

(v) Undertake socio-economic policies that promote sustainable development and support and ensure poverty eradication programmes, especially for women, by, inter alia, providing skills training, equal access to and control over resources, finance, credit, including microcredit, information and technology and equal access to markets to benefit women of all ages, in particular those living in poverty and marginalized women, including rural women, indigenous women and female-headed households;

(w) Take measures to develop and implement gender-sensitive programmes aimed at stimulating women's entrepreneurship and private initiative and assist women-owned business in participating in and benefiting from, inter alia, international trade, technological innovation and investment;

(x) Develop strategies to increase employment of women and to ensure that women, including women living in poverty, are protected by law against discriminatory terms and conditions of employment and any form of exploitation, that they benefit fully from job creation through a balanced representation of women and men in all sectors and occupations and that women receive equal pay for equal work or work of equal value to diminish differentials in incomes between women and men;

(y) Facilitate the transfer to developing countries and countries with economies in transition of appropriate technology, particularly new and modern technology, and encourage efforts by the international community to eliminate restrictions on such transfers as an effective means of complementing national efforts for further acceleration in achieving the goals of gender equality, development and peace;

(z) Promote and facilitate the equal access of women and girls, including those living in rural areas, to information and communications technologies, including newly developed technologies, and promote women's and girls' access to education and training in their use, access to, investment and use of these technologies for, inter alia, networking, advocacy, exchange of information, business, education, media consultation and e-commerce initiatives;

(aa) Ensure that national legislative and administrative reform processes, including those linked to land reform, decentralization and reorientation of the economy, promote the rights of women, particularly those of rural women and women living in poverty, and take measures to promote and implement those rights through women's equal access to and control over economic resources, including land, property rights, the right to inheritance, credit and traditional saving schemes, such as women's banks and cooperatives;

(bb) Ensure that clean water is available and accessible to all, particularly to women living in poverty;

(cc) Provide additional international financing and assistance to developing countries in support of their efforts to empower women and eradicate poverty and mainstream gender perspectives in the official development assistance process, including specific provisions for meeting the needs of women living in poverty in areas such as education, training, employment and health, as well as in social and economic policies, including macroeconomic policies, with a view of achieving sustainable development, and urge developed countries that have not done so to make concrete efforts towards the target of 0.7 per cent of gross national product (GNP) as official development assistance to developing countries and 0.15 to 0.20 per cent of GNP of developed countries to least developed countries, as reconfirmed at the Third United Nations Conference on Least Developed Countries, and encourage developing countries to build on progress achieved in ensuring that official development assistance is used effectively to help to achieve development goals and targets;

(dd) Promote, in the spirit of solidarity, international cooperation, including through voluntary contributions, in order to undertake actions in the field of poverty eradication, particularly among women and girls;

(ee) Ensure that women, especially poor women in developing countries, benefit from the pursuit of effective, equitable, development-oriented and durable solutions to the external debt and debt-servicing problems of developing countries, including the option of official development assistance debt cancellation, and call for continued international cooperation;

(*ff*) Forge constructive partnerships among Governments, non-governmental organizations, the private sector and other stakeholders to promote gender equality and the empowerment of women in poverty eradication efforts and to further support and encourage women and men, girls and boys, to form new advocacy networks and alliances.

6.   The Commission on the Status of Women welcomes the convening of the International Conference on Financing for Development, and underlines the importance of its objectives in relation to gender equality, the empowerment of women and poverty eradication.

7.   The Commission on the Status of Women also welcomes the convening of the Second World Assembly on Ageing, stresses the importance of mainstreaming a gender perspective into the preparations, work and outcome of the Assembly, including the Political Declaration and Madrid International Plan of Action on Ageing, 2002,[69] and welcomes the involvement of all women in the work of the Assembly, and the inclusion of women in delegations to the Assembly. Recognition should be given to the contribution of older women and special attention paid to their empowerment and well-being.

8.   The Commission on the Status of Women further welcomes the convening of the World Summit on Sustainable Development, stresses the importance of mainstreaming a gender perspective and of the involvement of women in the preparations, work and outcome of the World Summit, and encourages the inclusion of women in delegations to the Summit.

Agreed conclusions 2002/5B

Environmental management and the mitigation of natural disasters

1.   The Commission on the Status of Women recalls that, in the Beijing Declaration and Platform for Action,[70] it was recognized that environmental degradation and disasters affect all human lives and often have a more direct impact on women and that it was recommended that the role of

---

[69]   *Report of the Second World Assembly on Ageing, Madrid, 8-2 April 2002* (United Nations publication, Sales No. E.02.IV.4), chap. I, resolution 1, annexes I and II.

[70]   *Report of the Fourth World Conference on Women ...*

women and the environment be further investigated. The twenty-third special session of the General Assembly identified natural disasters as a current challenge affecting the full implementation of the Platform for Action and emphasized the need to incorporate a gender perspective in the development and implementation of disaster prevention, mitigation and recovery strategies. The Commission also recalls the resolve in the United Nations Millennium Declaration[71] to intensify cooperation to reduce the number and effects of natural and man-made disasters, as well as General Assembly resolution 46/182 of 19 December 1991, the annex to which contained the guiding principles of humanitarian assistance.

2.   Deeply convinced that economic development, social development and environmental protection are interdependent and mutually reinforcing components of sustainable development, which is the framework for our efforts to achieve a higher quality of life for all people.

3.   The Commission reiterates the strategic objectives and actions adopted by the Fourth World Conference on Women, held in Beijing in 1995,[72] and in the outcome document of the twenty-third special session of the General Assembly entitled "Women 2000: gender equality, development and peace for the twenty-first century", held in New York in 2000.[73]

4.   The Commission recognizes that women play a vital role in disaster reduction (prevention, mitigation and preparedness), response and recovery and in natural resources management, that disaster situations aggravate vulnerable conditions and that some women face particular vulnerabilities in this context.

5.   The Commission also recognizes that women's strengths in dealing with disasters and supporting their families and communities should be built upon following disasters to rebuild and restore their communities and mitigate against future disasters.

6.   The Commission further recognizes the need to enhance women's capacities and institutional mechanisms to respond to disasters in order to enhance gender equality and the empowerment of women.

7.   The Commission urges Governments and, as appropriate, also urges the relevant funds and programmes, organizations and the specialized agencies of the United Nations system, the international financial institutions, civil society, including the private sector and non-governmental organizations, and other stakeholders to take the following actions to accelerate implementation of these strategic objectives to address the needs of all women:

---

[71]   See General Assembly resolution 55/2.

[72]   *Report of the Fourth World Conference on Women ...*

[73]   General Assembly resolution S23/3, annex.

(*a*) Pursue gender equality and gender-sensitive environmental management and disaster reduction, response and recovery as an integral part of sustainable development;

(*b*) Take measures to integrate a gender perspective in the design and implementation of, among other things, environmentally sound and sustainable resource and disaster management mechanisms and establish mechanisms to review such efforts;

(*c*) Ensure the full participation of women in sustainable development decision-making and disaster reduction management at all levels;

(*d*) Ensure the full enjoyment by women and girls of all human rights—civil, cultural, economic, political and social, including the right to development—including in disaster reduction, response and recovery; in this context, special attention should be given to the prevention and prosecution of gender-based violence;

(*e*) Mainstream a gender perspective into ongoing research by, inter alia, the academic sector on the impact of climate change, natural hazards, disasters and related environmental vulnerability, including their root causes, and encourage the application of the results of this research in policies and programmes;

(*f*) Collect demographic and socio-economic data and information disaggregated by sex and age, develop national gender-sensitive indicators and analyse gender differences with regard to environmental management, disaster occurrence and associated losses and risks and vulnerability reduction;

(*g*) Develop, review and implement, as appropriate, with the involvement and participation of women's groups, gender-sensitive laws, policies and programmes, including on land-use and urbanization planning, natural resource and environmental management and integrated water resources management, to provide opportunities to prevent and mitigate damage;

(*h*) Encourage, as appropriate, the development and implementation of national building standards that take into account natural hazards so that women, men and their families are not exposed to high risk from disasters;

(*i*) Include gender analysis and methods of mapping hazards and vulnerabilities at the design stage of all relevant development programmes and projects in order to improve the effectiveness of disaster risk management, involving women and men equally;

(*j*) Ensure women's equal access to information and formal and non-formal education on disaster reduction, including through gender-sensitive early warning systems, and empower women to take related action in a timely and appropriate manner;

(k) Promote income-generating activities and employment opportunities, including through the provision of microcredit and other financial instruments, ensure equal access to resources, in particular land and property ownership, including housing, and take measures to empower women as producers and consumers, in order to enhance the capacity of women to respond to disasters;

(l) Design and implement gender-sensitive economic relief and recovery projects and ensure equal economic opportunities for women, including in both the formal and the non-formal sectors, taking into account the loss of land and property, including housing and other productive and personal assets;

(m) Make women full and equal partners in the development of safer communities and in determining national or local priorities for disaster reduction and incorporate local and indigenous knowledge, skills and capacities into environmental management and disaster reduction;

(n) Support capacity-building at all levels aimed at disaster reduction, based on knowledge about women's and men's needs and opportunities;

(o) Introduce formal and non-formal education and training programmes at all levels, including in the areas of science, technology and economics, with an integrated and gender-sensitive approach to environmentally sound and sustainable resource management and disaster reduction, response and recovery in order to change behaviour and attitudes in rural and urban areas;

(p) Ensure the implementation of their commitments by all Governments made in Agenda 21[74] and the Beijing Platform for Action[75] and the outcome document of the twenty-third special session of the General Assembly, including those in the areas of financial and technical assistance and the transfer of environmentally sound technologies to the developing countries, and ensure that a gender perspective is mainstreamed into all such assistance and transfers;

(q) Document good practice and lessons learned, particularly from effective community-based strategies for disaster reduction,

---

[74] *Report of the United Nations Conference on Environment and Development, Rio de Janeiro, 3-14 June 1992* (United Nations publication, Sales No. E.93.I.8 and corrigenda), vol. I: *Resolutions adopted by the Conference*, resolution 1, annex II.

[75] *Report of the Fourth World Conference on Women ...*

response and recovery, which actively involve women as well as men, and widely disseminate this information to all stakeholders;

(r) Improve and develop physical and mental health programmes, services and social support networks for women who suffer from the effects of natural disasters, including trauma;

(s) Strengthen the capacities of ministries, emergency authorities, practitioners and communities to apply a gender-sensitive approach to environmental management and disaster reduction and the involvement of women professionals and field workers;

(t) Forge constructive partnerships between Governments, international organizations and civil society, including the private sector and non-governmental organizations, and other stakeholders in integrated and gender-sensitive sustainable development initiatives to reduce environmental risks;

(u) Encourage civil society, including non-governmental organizations, to mainstream a gender perspective in the promotion of sustainable development initiatives, including in disaster reduction;

(v) Ensure coordination in the United Nations system, including the full and active participation of funds, programmes and specialized agencies to mainstream a gender perspective in sustainable development including, inter alia, environmental management and disaster reduction activities.

8.   The Commission on the Status of Women calls for the integration of a gender perspective in the implementation of all policies and treaties related to sustainable development and in the review of the implementation of the Yokohama Strategy for a Safer World: Guidelines for Natural Disaster Prevention, Preparedness and Mitigation and its Plan of Action, scheduled for 2004.

9.   The Commission on the Status of Women welcomes the International Strategy for Disaster Reduction efforts to mainstream a gender perspective in the mitigation of disasters.

10.   The Commission on the Status of Women welcomes also the policy statement of the Inter-Agency Standing Committee for the integration of a gender perspective in humanitarian assistance, of 31 May 1999.

11.   The Commission on the Status of Women welcomes further the convening of the International Conference on Financing for Development[76]

---

[76]   *Report of the International Conference on Financing for Development, Monterrey, Mexico, 18-22 March 2002* (United Nations publication, Sales No. E.02.II.A.7), chap. I, resolution 1, annex.

and takes note of the recognition, contained in the Monterrey Consensus, of the particular needs of women and the importance of gender equality and the empowerment of women, as well as the recognition of the impact of disasters.

12.   The Commission on the Status of Women welcomes the convening of the World Summit on Sustainable Development in Johannesburg, South Africa, stresses the importance of gender mainstreaming throughout the process and urges gender balance in the composition of delegations as well as the involvement and full participation of women in the preparations, work and outcome of the World Summit, thus renewing the commitment to gender equality objectives at the international level. The Commission on the Status of Women further reiterates that all States and all people shall cooperate in the essential task of eradicating poverty as an indispensable requirement for sustainable development, in order to decrease the disparities in standards of living and better meet the needs of the majority of the people of the world.

Forty-seventh session[77]
3-14 and 25 March 2003

Agreed conclusions:

2003/44. **Participation in and access of women to the media, and information and communication technologies and their impact on and use as an instrument for the advancement and empowerment of women**

The agreed conclusions adopted for the forty-seventh session of the Commission on the Status of Women can be found in *Resolutions and decisions adopted by the Economic and Social Council at its substantive session of 2003* (E/2003/INF/2/Add.4), resolution 2003/44.

---

[77] The Commission also considered the critical area of concern, women's human rights and the elimination of all forms of violence against women and girls as defined in the Beijing Platform for Action and the outcome documents of the special session of the General Assembly, entitled "Women 2000: gender equality, development and peace for the twenty-first century". No agreed conclusions were adopted.

Agreed conclusions 2003/44
Participation in and access of women to the media, and information and communication technologies and their impact on and use as an instrument for the advancement and empowerment of women

1.   The Commission on the Status of Women recalls and reiterates the strategic objectives and actions of the Beijing Declaration and Platform for Action[78] and the outcome document adopted at the twenty-third special session of the General Assembly entitled "Gender equality, development and peace in the twenty-first century",[79] on the potential of the media and of information and communications technologies to contribute to the advancement and empowerment of women. It also recalls the United Nations Millennium Declaration[80] and its Development Goals to promote gender equality and the empowerment of women as effective ways to combat poverty, hunger and disease, to stimulate development that is truly sustainable and to ensure that the benefits of new technologies, especially information and communications technologies, are available to all.

2.   The Commission notes that, globally, there are substantial differences in participation in, access to and use of media and information and communications technologies, their content and production. Such differences have important implications for policy development at national, regional and international levels. A focus on the gender dimensions of information and communications technologies is essential in order to prevent and combat any adverse impact of the digital revolution on gender equality and the perpetuation of existing inequalities and discrimination, including the sexual exploitation of women both through the traditional media and new technologies. The media and information and communication technologies also offer tools for enhancing women's full access to the benefits of information and new technologies and can become central tools for women's empowerment and the promotion of gender equality. Efforts are therefore necessary to increase women's access to and participation in the media and information and communication technologies, including in their decision-making processes and new opportunities created through information and communication technologies.

---

[78]   *Report of the Fourth World Conference on Women ...*

[79]   General Assembly resolution S-23/3, annex.

[80]   General Assembly resolution 55/2.

3.   The Commission welcomes the convening of the World Summit on the Information Society, which is to be held in Geneva in December 2003 and in Tunis in 2005, and urges all participants to take the following recommendations into account and to integrate gender perspectives in every facet of the Summit. It further encourages the participation of women in the Summit, to include significant numbers of gender equality experts and women experts in the field of information and communication technology as members of national delegations, organizations of civil society and the business community.

4.   The Commission urges Governments and, as appropriate, the relevant funds and programmes, organizations and specialized agencies of the United Nations system, the international financial institutions, civil society, including the private sector and non-governmental organizations, and other stakeholders, to take the following actions:

   (a)   Prioritize the integration of gender perspectives and ensure women's early and full participation in the development and implementation of national policies, legislation, programmes, projects, strategies and regulatory and technical instruments in the field of information and communication technologies (ICT) and media and communications, and create monitoring and accountability mechanisms to ensure implementation of gender-sensitive policies and regulations as well as to analyse the gender impact of such policies in consultation and collaboration with women information technology specialists, women's organizations and gender-equality advocates;

   (b)   Encourage regulatory bodies, where they exist, to promote full participation of women in the ownership, control and management in the ICT and media sectors;

   (c)   Include gender perspectives and measurable gender-specific targets in all programmes and projects on ICT for development, as well as specific activities, as appropriate, for women and girls as active users of information;

   (d)   Remove ICT-related infrastructural barriers that disproportionately affect women and girls and promote the establishment of affordable and accessible ICT-related infrastructure for all women and girls, bearing in mind the specific needs and interests of women and girls living in countries in the process of peace-building and reconstruction;

   (e)   Invite, as appropriate, through partnerships, or through the use of self-regulatory gender-sensitive guidelines and self-regulatory gender-sensitive guidelines for media coverage and representation, public and community media to work in support of gender equality, bearing in mind the importance of providing financial resources and other support;

(*f*) Support research into all aspects of the impact of the media and ICT on women and girls, in particular into their information needs and interests, review existing media and ICT policies and find ways to adapt ICT to the needs of poor and, in particular, illiterate women, in order to overcome barriers and support women's empowerment;

(*g*) Make education, formal and non-formal, a priority in particular for the development of ICT and take measures to promote girls' education so as to enable girls and women to gain access to ICT;

(*h*) Include, at appropriate levels of government, ICT education for girls and women in curricula at all educational levels, from early childhood to tertiary level, as well as in continuing education, in order to promote and ensure women's full participation in the information society;

(*i*) Take concrete steps to increase the number of female students at all educational levels in media- and ICT-related subjects, including science, mathematics and technology, including through such methods as distance- and e-learning;

(*j*) Establish or, where they already exist, expand skills training, vocational and employment training and capacity-building programmes for women and girls and women's non-governmental organizations on the use, design and production of ICT, including preparing them to take on leadership roles and promote their participation in the political process, and integrate a gender perspective in ICT training programmes for teachers and in training programmes for media professionals;

(*k*) Enable equal access for women to ICT-based economic activities, such as small business and home-based employment, to information systems and improved technologies and to new employment opportunities in this area, and consider developing tele-centres, information centres, community access points and business incubators;

(*l*) Strengthen partnerships among all stakeholders to build the capacity of women to participate fully in, and enjoy the benefits of, the information society, including e-governance, where it exists and as it is developed, and participatory approaches;

(*m*) Ensure equal opportunities for women and monitor gender representation in different categories and levels of work, education and training in the media and ICT areas, with a view to increasing women's participation in decision-making at all levels of ICT and the media;

(*n*) Provide management, negotiation and leadership training for women, as well as mentoring systems and other support strategies and programmes to enhance women's capabilities and potential for advancement in the media and ICT sectors;

(*o*) Take effective measures, to the extent consistent with freedom of expression, to combat the growing sexualization and use of pornography in media content, in terms of the rapid development of ICT, encourage the media to refrain from presenting women as inferior beings and exploiting them as sexual objects and commodities, combat ICT- and media-based violence against women, including criminal misuse of ICT for sexual harassment, sexual exploitation and trafficking in women and girls, and support the development and use of ICT as a resource for the empowerment of women and girls, including those affected by violence, abuse and other forms of sexual exploitation;

(*p*) Respect the value of different and local languages and promote and encourage local knowledge systems and locally produced content in media and communications, support the development of a wide range of ICT-based programmes in local languages, as appropriate, with content relevant to different groups of women, and build the capacity of girls and women to develop ICT content;

(*q*) Encourage South-South cooperation to facilitate transfer and exchange of low-cost technologies and appropriate ICT content between developing countries for the benefit of women and girls;

(*r*) Strengthen and encourage the use of existing information and communication technologies, such as radio, television, telecommunications and print, in parallel, in order to enhance the use of new technologies for gender equality and the economic, political and social empowerment of women as leaders, participants and consumers and recognize that women and girls are potentially large-scale consumers, users and producers of ICT and media;

(*s*) Collect, share, positively recognize and widely publicize good practices to counter gender stereotyping, negative portrayals and exploitation of women in all forms of the media and ICT as part of their efforts to eliminate discrimination and violence against women;

(*t*) Increase efforts to compile, and disaggregate by sex and age, statistics on ICT use, in order to develop gender-specific indicators on ICT use and needs and to collect gender-specific data on employment and education patterns in the media and in ICT professions;

(*u*) Provide adequate and appropriate resources for innovative, affordable, accessible and sustainable media and ICT programmes, projects and products that support gender equality and gender mainstreaming, are relevant to the concerns of women and girls and provide support to women's online communities and networks that promote gender equality;

(*v*) Prioritize the allocation of resources to support programmes, projects and strategies that aim at increasing women's participation in, and equal access to, the information society, including vocational, scientific and technical training, literacy training and capacity-building programmes;

(*w*) Enhance, for the benefit of women and girls, international cooperation in support of national efforts to create an enabling environment to reduce the digital and information divide between developed and developing countries and promote, develop and enhance access to ICT, including the Internet infrastructure by facilitating access to, and transfer of, knowledge and technology on concessional, preferential and favourable terms to the developing countries, as mutually agreed, taking into account the need to protect intellectual property rights and the special needs of developing countries;

(*x*) Strengthen the capacity of national machineries for the advancement of women, including through the allocation of adequate and appropriate resources and the provision of technical expertise, to take a lead advocacy role with respect to media and ICT and gender equality, support their involvement in national, regional and international processes related to media and ICT issues and enhance coordination among ministries responsible for ICT, national machineries for the advancement of women, the private sector and national non-governmental organizations working in the field of gender advocacy.

Forty-eighth session
1-12 March 2004

Agreed conclusions:

2004/11. **The role of men and boys in achieving gender equality**

2004/12. **Women's equal participation in conflict prevention, management and resolution and in post-conflict peacebuilding**

The agreed conclusions adopted for the forty-eighth session of the Commission on the Status of Women can be found in the *Resolutions and decisions adopted by the Economic and Social Council at its substantive session of 2004* (E/2004/INF/2/Add.2), resolutions 2004/11 and 2004/12.

Agreed conclusions 2004/11

The role of men and boys in achieving gender equality

The Economic and Social Council

Endorses the following agreed conclusions adopted by the Commission on the Status of Women at its forty-eighth session with respect to the role of men and boys in achieving gender equality:

1.   The Commission on the Status of Women recalls and reiterates that the Beijing Declaration[81] and Platform for Action[82] encouraged men to participate fully in all actions towards gender equality and urged the establishment of the principle of shared power and responsibility between women and men at home, in the community, in the workplace and in the wider national and international communities. The Commission also recalls and reiterates the outcome document[83] adopted at the twenty-third special session of the General Assembly entitled "Women 2000: gender equality, development and peace in the twenty-first century", which emphasized that men must take joint responsibility with women for the promotion of gender equality.

2.   The Commission recognizes that while men and boys sometimes face discriminatory barriers and practices, they can and do make contributions to gender equality in many capacities, including as individuals and as members of families, social groups and communities, in all spheres of society.

3.   The Commission recognizes that gender inequalities still exist and are reflected in imbalances of power between women and men in all spheres of society. The Commission further recognizes that everyone benefits from gender equality and that the negative impacts of gender inequality are borne by society as a whole and emphasizes, therefore, that men and boys, through taking responsibility themselves and working jointly in partnership with women and girls, are essential to the achievement of the goals of gender equality, development and peace. The Commission recognizes the capacity of men and boys to bring about change in attitudes, relationships and access to resources and decision-making, which are critical for the promotion of gender equality and the full enjoyment of all human rights by women.

4.   The Commission acknowledges and encourages men and boys to continue to take positive initiatives to eliminate gender stereotypes and

---

[81]   *Report of the Fourth World Conference on Women ...*

[82]   Ibid.

[83]   General Assembly resolution S-23/3, annex.

promote gender equality, including combating violence against women, through networks, peer programmes, information campaigns and training programmes. The Commission acknowledges the critical role of gender-sensitive education and training in achieving gender equality.

5.   The Commission also recognizes that the participation of men and boys in achieving gender equality must be consistent with the empowerment of women and girls, and acknowledges that efforts must be made to address the undervaluation of many types of work, abilities and roles associated with women. In this regard, it is important that resources for gender equality initiatives for men and boys do not compromise equal opportunities and resources for women and girls.

6.   The Commission urges Governments and, as appropriate, the relevant funds, programmes and organizations and the specialized agencies of the United Nations system, the international financial institutions, civil society, including the private sector and non-governmental organizations, and other stakeholders to take the following actions:

(*a*) Encourage and support the capacity of men and boys to foster gender equality, including by acting in partnership with women and girls as agents for change and providing positive leadership, in particular where men are still key decision makers, responsible for policies, programmes and legislation, as well as holders of economic and organizational power and public resources;

(*b*) Promote understanding of the importance of fathers, mothers, legal guardians and other caregivers for the well-being of children and the promotion of gender equality, and the need to develop policies, programmes and school curricula that encourage and maximize their positive involvement in achieving gender equality and positive results for children, families and communities;

(*c*) Create and improve training and education programmes to enhance awareness and knowledge among men and women of their roles as parents, legal guardians and caregivers and the importance of sharing family responsibilities, and include fathers as well as mothers in programmes that teach infant childcare and development;

(*d*) Develop and include in education programmes for parents, legal guardians and other caregivers information on ways and means to increase the capacity of men to raise children in a manner oriented towards gender equality;

(*e*) Encourage men and boys to work with women and girls in the design of policies and programmes for men and boys aimed at gender equality, and foster the involvement of men and boys in gender mainstreaming efforts in order to ensure improved design of all policies and programmes;

(*f*) Encourage the design and implementation of programmes at all levels to accelerate a sociocultural change towards gender equality, especially through the upbringing and educational process and by changing harmful traditional perceptions of and attitudes regarding male and female roles in order to achieve the full and equal participation of women and men in society;

(*g*) Develop and implement programmes for pre-schools, schools, community centres, youth organizations, sport clubs and centres and other groups dealing with children and youth, including training for teachers, social workers and other professionals who deal with children, in order to foster positive attitudes and behaviour with regard to gender equality;

(*h*) Promote critical reviews of school curricula, textbooks and other information, education and communication materials at all levels in order to recommend ways to strengthen the promotion of gender equality that involves the engagement of boys as well as girls;

(*i*) Develop and implement strategies to educate boys and girls and men and women about tolerance, mutual respect for all individuals and the promotion of all human rights;

(*j*) Develop and utilize a variety of methods in public information campaigns on the role of men and boys in promoting gender equality, including through approaches specifically targeting boys and young men;

(*k*) Engage media, advertising and other related professionals, through the development of training and other programmes, on the importance of promoting gender equality, the non-stereotypical portrayal of women and girls and men and boys and on the harm caused by portraying women and girls in a demeaning or exploitative manner, as well as on the enhanced participation of women and girls in the media;

(*l*) Take effective measures, to the extent consistent with freedom of expression, to combat the growing sexualization of, and use of pornography in, media content and in the rapid development of information and communications technology, encourage men in the media to refrain from presenting women as inferior beings and exploiting them as sexual objects and commodities, combat information and communications technology- and media-based violence against women, including criminal misuse of information and communications technology for sexual harassment, sexual exploitation and trafficking in women and girls, and support the development and use of such technology as a resource for the empowerment of women and girls, including those affected by violence, abuse and other forms of sexual exploitation;

(*m*) Adopt and implement legislation and/or policies to close the gap between women's and men's pay, and promote reconciliation of occupational and family responsibilities, including through the reduction of occupational segregation, the introduction or expansion of parental leave, and flexible working arrangements, such as voluntary part-time work, teleworking and other home-based work;

(*n*) Encourage men, through training and education, to participate fully in the care and support of others, including older persons, persons with disabilities and sick persons, in particular children and other dependants;

(*o*) Encourage the active involvement of men and boys, through education projects and peer-based programmes, in eliminating gender stereotypes as well as gender inequality, in particular in relation to sexually transmitted infections, including HIV/AIDS, as well as their full participation in prevention, advocacy, care, treatment, support and impact evaluation programmes;

(*p*) Ensure men's access to and utilization of reproductive and sexual health services and programmes, including HIV/AIDS-related programmes and services, and encourage men to participate with women in programmes designed to prevent the transmission and treat all forms of HIV/AIDS and other sexually transmitted infections;

(*q*) Design and implement programmes to encourage and enable men to adopt safe and responsible sexual and reproductive behaviour and to use effectively methods to prevent unwanted pregnancies and sexually transmitted infections, including HIV/AIDS;

(*r*) Encourage and support men and boys to take an active part in the prevention and elimination of all forms of violence, especially gender-based violence, including in the context of HIV/AIDS, and increase awareness of men's and boys' responsibility in ending the cycle of violence, inter alia, through the promotion of attitudinal and behavioural change, integrated education and training prioritizing the safety of women and children, the prosecution and rehabilitation of perpetrators of violence and support for survivors, recognizing that men and boys also experience violence;

(*s*) Encourage increased understanding among men of how violence, including trafficking for the purposes of commercialized sexual exploitation, forced marriage and forced labour, harms women,

men and children and undermines gender equality, and consider measures aimed at eliminating the demand for trafficked women and children;

(*t*) Encourage and support both women and men in leadership positions, including political leaders, traditional leaders, business leaders, community and religious leaders, musicians, artists and athletes, to provide positive role models of gender equality;

(*u*) Encourage men in leadership positions to ensure equal access for women to education, property rights and inheritance rights and to promote equal access to information technology and business and economic opportunities, including in international trade, in order to provide women with the tools to enable them to take part fully and equally in economic and political decision-making processes at all levels;

(*v*) Identify and fully utilize all contexts in which a large number of men can be reached, particularly in male-dominated institutions, industries and associations, in order to sensitize men on their roles and responsibilities in the promotion of gender equality and the full enjoyment of all human rights by women, including in relation to HIV/AIDS and violence against women;

(*w*) Develop and use statistics to support and/or carry out research, inter alia, on the cultural, social and economic conditions that influence the attitudes and behaviour of men and boys towards women and girls, their awareness of gender inequalities and their involvement in promoting gender equality;

(*x*) Carry out research on the views of men and boys on gender equality and their perceptions of their roles, through which further programmes and policies can be developed, identify and widely disseminate good practices, and assess the impact of efforts undertaken to engage men and boys in achieving gender equality;

(*y*) Promote and encourage the representation of men in institutional mechanisms for the advancement of women;

(*z*) Encourage men and boys to support the equal participation of women in conflict prevention, management and resolution and in post-conflict peacebuilding;

7. The Commission urges all entities within the United Nations system to take into account the recommendations contained in the present agreed conclusions and to disseminate the agreed conclusions widely.

Agreed conclusions 2004/12

Women's equal participation in conflict prevention, management and resolution and in post-conflict peacebuilding

1.   The Commission on the Status of Women recalls and reiterates the strategic objectives and actions of the Beijing Declaration[84] and Platform for Action,[85] the outcome document of the twenty-third special session of the General Assembly, entitled "Gender equality, development and peace for the twenty-first century",[86] and its agreed conclusions on women and armed conflict adopted at its forty-second session in 1998. It also recalls the Convention on the Elimination of All Forms of Discrimination against Women,[87] Security Council resolution 1325 (2000) on women, peace and security and all relevant resolutions of the General Assembly, including resolution 58/142 of 22 December 2003 on women and political participation.

2.   The Commission calls for the full respect of international human rights law and international humanitarian law, including the four Geneva Conventions of 1949,[88] in particular the Fourth Geneva Convention relative to the Protection of Civilian Persons in Time of War.

3.   The Commission calls for the promotion and protection of the full enjoyment of all human rights and fundamental freedoms by women and girls at all times, including during conflict prevention, conflict management and conflict resolution and in post-conflict peacebuilding. It further calls for protection and security for women and girls under threat of violence and their freedom of movement and participation in social, political and economic activities.

4.   The Commission recognizes that the root causes of armed conflict are multidimensional in nature and thus require a comprehensive and integrated approach to the prevention of armed conflict.

5.   International cooperation based on the principles of the Charter of the United Nations enhances women's full and equal participation in conflict prevention, conflict management and conflict resolution and in post-conflict peacebuilding and contributes to the promotion of sustainable and durable peace.

---

[84]   *Report of the Fourth World Conference on Women* ...

[85]   Ibid.

[86]   General Assembly resolution S-23/3, annex.

[87]   General Assembly resolution 34/180, annex.

[88]   United Nations, *Treaty Series*, vol. 75, Nos. 970-973.

6.   To achieve sustainable and durable peace, the full and equal participation of women and girls and the integration of gender perspectives in all aspects of conflict prevention, management and resolution and in post-conflict peacebuilding is essential. Yet women continue to be underrepresented in the processes, institutions and mechanisms dealing with these areas. Further effort is therefore needed to promote gender equality and ensure women's equal participation at all levels of decision-making in all relevant institutions. Further effort, including consideration of adequate resourcing, is also needed to build and consolidate the capacity of women and women's groups to participate fully in these processes, as well as to promote understanding of the essential role of women. In this regard, the international community should use lessons learned from actual experience to identify and overcome barriers to women's equal participation.

7.   The Commission recognizes that while both men and women suffer from the consequences of armed conflict, there is a differential impact on women and girls, who are often subject to, and affected by, particular forms of violence and deprivation. The Commission calls for measures to prevent gender-based violence, including sexual violence against women and girls, as well as trafficking in human beings, especially trafficking in women and girls, arising from armed conflict and in post-conflict situations and to prosecute perpetrators of such crimes.

8.   The Commission encourages the collection and dissemination of sex-disaggregated data and information for planning, evaluation and analysis in order to promote the mainstreaming of a gender perspective into conflict prevention, management and resolution and in post-conflict peacebuilding.

9.   Peace agreements provide a vehicle for the promotion of gender equality and the participation of women in post-conflict situations. Significant opportunities for women's participation arise in the preparatory phase leading up to a peace agreement. The content of a peace agreement likewise offers significant scope for ensuring that the rights, concerns and priorities of women and girls are fully addressed. Finally, once a peace agreement has been concluded, its implementation should be pursued with explicit attention to women's full and equal participation and the goal of gender equality.

10.   Women's full and equal participation and the integration of gender perspectives are crucial to democratic electoral processes in post-conflict situations. A gender-sensitive constitutional and legal framework, especially electoral laws and regulations, is necessary to ensure that women can fully participate in such processes. Political parties can play a crucial role in promoting women's equal participation. Steps are also necessary to ensure that women participate fully in, and that a gender perspective is incorporated throughout, the design and implementation of voter and civic education programmes and in election administration and observation.

11.   Governments in particular, as well as the United Nations system, especially those United Nations entities having a mandate with regard to peace and security, and other relevant international, regional and national actors, including civil society, have a responsibility for advancing gender equality and ensuring women's full and equal participation in all aspects of peace processes and in post-conflict peace-building, reconstruction, rehabilitation and reconciliation, where they are participants in these processes.

12.   In regard to conflict prevention, the Commission on the Status of Women calls on Governments, as well as all other relevant participants in these processes:

(a)   To improve the collection, analysis and inclusion of information on women and gender issues as part of conflict prevention and early warning efforts;

(b)   To ensure better collaboration and coordination between efforts to promote gender equality and efforts aimed at conflict prevention;

(c)   To support capacity-building, especially for civil society, in particular for women's organizations, in order to increase community commitment to conflict prevention;

(d)   To continue to make resources available nationally and internationally for the prevention of conflict and ensure women's participation in the elaboration and implementation of strategies for preventing conflict.

13.   In regard to peace processes, the Commission on the Status of Women calls on Governments, as well as all other relevant participants in these processes:

(a)   To promote women's full, equal and effective participation as actors in all peace processes, in particular negotiation, mediation and facilitation;

(b)   To ensure that peace agreements address, from a gender perspective, the full range of security aspects, including legal, political, social, economic and physical, and also address the specific needs and priorities of women and girls;

(c)   To ensure, in the implementation phase of a peace agreement, that all provisions concerning gender equality and the participation of women are fully complied with and that all provisions of the peace agreement, including those concerning demobilization, disarmament, reintegration and rehabilitation, are implemented in a manner that promotes gender equality and ensures women's full and equal participation;

(*d*) To promote women's full and equal access to public information relative to peace processes;

(*e*) To review, on a regular basis, their contributions to the promotion of gender equality and the full and equal participation of women, and to fulfil their monitoring, accountability and reporting obligations in the implementation of peace agreements;

(*f*) With regard to gender mainstreaming, to ensure and support the full participation of women at all levels of decision-making and implementation in development activities and peace processes, including conflict prevention and resolution, post-conflict reconstruction, peacemaking, peacekeeping and peacebuilding and, in this regard, support the involvement of women's organizations, community-based organizations and non-governmental organizations;

(*g*) To develop and strengthen the provision of gender advisory capacity and gender sensitive-training programmes for all staff in missions relating to armed conflicts.

In this regard, the Commission takes note of the report of the Secretary-General.[89]

14. In regard to post-conflict peacebuilding, the Commission on the Status of Women calls on Governments, as well as all other relevant participants in these processes,

Concerning elections

(*a*) To ensure equal access of women in all stages of the electoral process and to consider the adoption of measures for increasing women's participation in elections through, inter alia, individual voter registration, temporary gender-specific positive actions and access to information, representation on bodies administering elections and as election monitors and observers, as well as encouraging political parties to involve women fully and equally in all aspects of their operations;

(*b*) To ensure equal access for women to voter and civic education, to provide women candidates with full support, training and financial resources and to eliminate discriminatory practices hampering women's participation either as voters or candidates.

Concerning reconstruction and rehabilitation

(*a*) To ensure the full participation of women on an equal basis in the reconstruction and rehabilitation process;

(*b*) To ensure the equal access of women to social services, in particular in the areas of health and education, and, in this regard, to

---

[89] E/CN.6/2004/10.

promote the provision of adequate health care and health services, assistance for women and girls in conflict and post-conflict situations and counselling for post-conflict trauma;

(c)　To facilitate equal employment opportunities for women to achieve economic empowerment.

15.　The realization and the achievement of the goals of gender equality, development and peace need to be supported by the allocation of the necessary human, financial and material resources for specific and targeted activities to ensure gender equality at the local, national, regional and international levels, as well as by enhanced and increased international cooperation.

16.　The Commission on the Status of Women requests the Secretary-General to disseminate the present agreed conclusions widely, including to the high-level panel on global security threats and reform of the international system.

Forty-ninth session
28 February–11 and 22 March 2005

No agreed conclusions were adopted.

The Commission adopted a Declaration (E/2005/27-E/CN.6/2005/11 and Corr.1) reaffirming the Beijing Declaration and Platform for Action and the outcome of the twenty-third special session of the General Assembly. The Declaration emphasized that the full and effective implementation of the Beijing Declaration and Platform for Action is essential to achieving the internationally agreed development goals, including those contained in the Millennium Declaration, and stressed the need to ensure the integration of a gender perspective in the high-level plenary meeting on the review of the Millennium Declaration. It also recognized that the Beijing Declaration and the Platform for Action and the Convention on the Elimination of All Forms of Discrimination against Women are mutually reinforcing in achieving gender equality and empowerment of women. The Declaration called upon the United Nations system and other actors to commit themselves fully and to intensify their contributions to the implementation of the Beijing Declaration and Platform for Action and the outcome of the twenty-third special session of the General Assembly.

The 10-year review and appraisal of the implementation of the Beijing Platform of Action and the outcome documents of the special session of the General Assembly entitled "Women 2000: gender equality, development and peace for the twenty-first century" were carried out during the forty-ninth session of the Commission on the Status of Women.

Fiftieth session

22 March 2005, 27 February–10 March and 16 March 2006

Agreed conclusions:

Enhanced participation of women in development: an enabling environment for achieving gender equality and the advancement of women, taking into account, inter alia, the fields of education, health and work

Equal participation of women and men in decision-making processes at all levels

The agreed conclusions adopted for the fiftieth session of the Commission on the Status of Women can be found in the *Official Records of the Economic and Social Council, 2006, Supplement No. 7* (E/2006/27-E/CN.6/2006/15, Corr.1 and 2).

Agreed conclusions

Enhanced participation of women in development: an enabling environment for achieving gender equality and the advancement of women, taking into account, inter alia, the fields of education, health and work

1.   The Commission on the Status of Women reaffirmed the Beijing Declaration and Platform for Action, the outcome documents of the twenty-third special session of the General Assembly entitled "Women 2000: gender equality, development and peace for the twenty-first century", the United Nations Millennium Declaration of 2000, the Declaration adopted by the Commission on the Status of Women on the occasion of the tenth anniversary of the Fourth World Conference on Women,[90] the 2005 World Summit,[91] as well as all relevant General Assembly resolutions and outcomes of United Nations conferences; reiterated that women's empowerment and their full participation on the basis of equality in all spheres of society, including participation in the decision-making process and access to power, were fundamental for the achievement of equality, development, peace and security; and emphasized the need to ensure the full integration and full participation of women as both agents and beneficiaries in the development process and its commitment to strengthening and safeguarding a national and international enabling environment, inter alia, through promoting and protecting all human rights and fundamental freedoms, mainstreaming a gender perspective into all policies and programmes, and promoting the full participation and empowerment of women and enhanced international cooperation.

2.   The Commission reaffirmed also that the full and effective implementation of the Beijing Declaration and Platform for Action was an essential contribution to achieving the internationally agreed development goals, including those contained in the Millennium Declaration, and that the promotion of gender equality and the empowerment of women was of fundamental importance in sustainable development, achieving sustained economic growth, eradicating poverty and hunger and combating diseases, and that investing in the development of women and girls had a multiplier effect,

---

[90]   *Official Records of the Economic and Social Council, 2005, Supplement No. 27* and corrigendum (E/2005/27 and Corr.1), chap. I.A.

[91]   See General Assembly resolution 60/1.

in particular on productivity, efficiency and sustained economic growth, in all sectors of the economy, especially in key areas such as agriculture, industry and services.

3. The Commission recalled that the Convention on the Elimination of All Forms of Discrimination against Women stressed that the full and complete development of a country, the welfare of the world and the cause of peace required the maximum participation of women on equal terms with men in all fields.

4. The Commission recognized that all forms of violence against women and girls violated the enjoyment of their human rights and constituted a major impediment to the ability of women and girls to make use of their capabilities, limiting their participation and agency in development, including in the achievement of the internationally agreed development goals, including the Millennium Development Goals.

5. The Commission recognized also that the creation of an enabling environment at all levels was necessary to enhance women's participation in and benefit from development processes, and that challenges to the creation of an enabling environment included:

(*a*) Insufficient coherence and coordination between development policies and gender-equality policies and strategies;

(*b*) Insufficient time-bound targets for implementation of gender-equality policies and strategies;

(*c*) Underrepresentation of women in decision-making;

(*d*) Insufficient promotion and protection of the full enjoyment by women of all human rights;

(*e*) Persistent violence and multiple forms of discriminatory practices and attitudes against women;

(*f*) Insufficient recognition of the contributions of women to the economy and to all areas of public life;

(*g*) Unequal access to education and training, health care and decent work;

(*h*) Unequal access to opportunities, and unequal access to and control over resources, such as land, credit, capital, economic assets, and information and communication technologies;

(*i*) Insufficient political will and resources;

(*j*) Inadequate implementation of gender mainstreaming;

(*k*) Insufficient national mechanisms for monitoring, evaluation and accountability;

(*l*) Impact on women of HIV/AIDS, malaria, tuberculosis and other communicable diseases;

(*m*) Armed conflicts, lack of security and natural disasters;

(*n*) Slow and uneven implementation of commitments to the internationally agreed development goals, including the Millennium Development Goals;

(*o*) Persistence of difficult socio-economic conditions that existed in many developing countries, which had resulted in the acceleration of the feminization of poverty;

(*p*) Insufficient international cooperation in the area of gender equality and empowerment of women in the context of poverty eradication and health, bearing in mind financing for development;

(*q*) Prevailing harmful cultural and traditional practices;

(*r*) Insufficient information and data and statistics disaggregated by sex;

(*s*) Insufficient progress in the promulgation of gender-responsive laws.

6. The Commission underlined that addressing such challenges at all levels required a systematic, comprehensive, integrated, multidisciplinary and multisectoral approach, with policy, legislative and programmatic interventions.

7. The Commission urged Governments and/or, as appropriate, the relevant entities of the United Nations system, other international and regional organizations, including the international financial institutions, national parliaments, political parties, and civil society, including the private sector, trade unions, academia, the media and non-governmental organizations and other actors, to take the following actions:

(*a*) Incorporate gender perspectives into all local and national planning, budgetary, monitoring and evaluation and reporting processes, and mechanisms relating to national development strategies, including strategies focused on the implementation of internationally agreed development goals, including the Millennium Development Goals, fully utilizing existing gender equality policies and strategies;

(*b*) Elaborate and implement comprehensive gender-sensitive poverty eradication strategies that addressed social, structural and macroeconomic issues;

(*c*) Develop and implement effective national monitoring and evaluation mechanisms at all levels to evaluate progress towards gender equality, including through the collection, compilation and analysis and use of data disaggregated by age and by sex and gender statistics, and continue developing and using appropriate qualitative and quantitative indicators;

(*d*) Encourage and promote close cooperation between central authorities and local governments to develop programmes aimed at the achievement of gender equality, thereby granting equal opportunities for women and girls;

(*e*) Elaborate and implement strategies and policies, including targeted measures in support of their obligation to exercise due diligence to prevent all forms of violence against women and girls, provide protection to victims and investigate, prosecute and punish perpetrators of such violence, and recognize that violence against women and girls was a serious obstacle to the achievement of the objectives of equality, development and peace and had a negative impact on the social and economic development of communities and States;

(*f*) Continue efforts towards full and effective implementation of General Assembly resolution 57/337 of 3 July 2003 on prevention of armed conflict, and its agreed conclusions on women's equal participation in conflict prevention, management and resolution and in post-conflict peacebuilding;[92]

(*g*) Continue efforts towards the full and effective implementation of Security Council resolution 1325 (2000) of 31 October 2000 on women and peace and security, recognizing the linkages between gender equality, peace, security and development;

(*h*) Take the necessary measures to ensure that women were accorded full and equal rights to own land and other property, including through inheritance;

(*i*) Take all appropriate measures to enable women to participate fully in decision-making at all levels in all aspects of their daily lives;

(*j*) Incorporate gender perspectives in all policies and programmes on international migration, promote the full enjoyment of human rights and fundamental freedoms by women migrants, combat discrimination, exploitation, ill-treatment, unsafe working conditions and violence, including sexual violence and trafficking, and facilitate family reunification in an expeditious and effective manner, with due regard to applicable laws, as such reunification had a positive effect on the integration of migrants;

(*k*) Eliminate all forms of discrimination, sexual exploitation and violence against female refugees, asylum-seekers and internally displaced persons and promote their active involvement in decisions affecting their lives and communities, while recalling the

---

[92]   Economic and Social Council resolution 2004/12.

relevant norms of international human rights law, international humanitarian law and international refugee law;

(*l*) Increase understanding of and capacity to implement gender mainstreaming as a strategy for achieving gender equality and women's empowerment, including by requiring the use of gender analysis as the basis for all policy and programme development, implementation, monitoring and evaluation, in particular in the areas of health, education and employment;

(*m*) Develop and promote strategies to mainstream a gender perspective into the design and implementation of development and socio-economic policies and budgetary processes, and share best practices and encourage innovations in gender mainstreaming approaches;

(*n*) Mobilize adequate funding for gender-sensitive development policies and programmes and for national mechanisms for gender equality, through national, regional and international resource mobilization and gender-responsive budget processes in all sector areas, and allocate adequate funding for women-specific measures;

(*o*) Support women's organizations that strive to empower women and girls and improve their living conditions;

(*p*) Encourage enhanced coordination and collaboration between all mechanisms for the advancement of women and gender-equality at all levels, such as women's ministries, gender-equality commissions, relevant parliamentary committees, ombudspersons, gender focal points and working groups in line ministries, as well as with women's groups, associations and networks;

(*q*) Take effective measures to eliminate discrimination, gender stereotypes and harmful traditional, cultural and customary practices;

(*r*) Develop and implement strategies to increase the involvement of men and boys in promoting gender equality and empowerment of women and girls through, inter alia, the elimination of all forms of violence against women and girls, the sharing of household work and family care, and the promotion of a culture of peace and tolerance, and encourage men and women to foster responsible sexual and reproductive behaviour and attitudinal changes to promote the realization of gender equality;

(*s*) Increase women's and girls' equal and effective access to and use of information and communication technologies, as well as applied technology, including through the transfer of knowledge and technology on concessional, preferential and favourable terms to developing countries, as mutually agreed, provision of training and infrastructure, involvement in the planning, development and production of content, and participation in management, governance and decision-making positions in regulatory or policymaking bodies for information and communication technologies;

(*t*) Invest in appropriate infrastructure and other projects, and create opportunities for economic empowerment in order to alleviate the burden of time-consuming everyday tasks on women and girls, allowing them, inter alia, to engage in income-generating activities and attend school;

(*u*) Give special attention to incorporating principles on advancing the equalization of opportunities in programmes, methods and processes to empower and support women and girls with disabilities;

(*v*) Call upon the international community to make efforts to mitigate the effects of excess volatility and economic disruption, which had a disproportionately negative impact on women, and to enhance trade opportunities for developing countries in order to improve the economic situation of women;

(*w*) Call upon States Parties to comply fully with their obligations under the Convention on the Elimination of All Forms of Discrimination against Women and the Optional Protocol thereto; take into consideration the concluding comments, as well as the general recommendations, of the Committee on the Elimination of Discrimination against Women; call upon other States Parties to the Convention that had not yet done so to consider signing, ratifying or acceding to the Optional Protocol thereto; and reinforce, in efforts to achieve the internationally agreed development goals, including the Millennium Development Goals, the linkages with the implementation of the Beijing Declaration and Platform for Action and the outcome of the twenty-third special session of the General Assembly, as well as with the Programme of Action of the International Conference on Population and Development and the key actions for the further implementation of the Programme of Action.

8. The Commission underlined the fact that each country had the primary responsibility for its own sustainable development and poverty eradication, that the role of national policies and development strategies could not be overemphasized, and that concerted and concrete measures were required at all levels to enable developing countries to eradicate poverty and achieve sustainable development.

9. The Commission urged Governments to ensure that women, especially poor women in developing countries, benefited from the pursuit

of effective, equitable, development-oriented and durable solutions to the external debt and debt-servicing problems of developing countries, including the option of official development assistance and debt cancellation, and called for continued international cooperation.

10. The Commission encouraged the international community, the United Nations system, the relevant regional and international organizations and the private sector and civil society to:

(a) Assist Governments, at their request, in building institutional capacity and developing national action plans or further implementing existing action plans for the implementation of the Beijing Platform for Action;

(b) Provide the necessary financial resources to assist national Governments in their efforts to meet the development targets and benchmarks agreed upon at the major United Nations summits and conferences and their follow-up processes, including the World Summit for Social Development, the Fourth World Conference on Women, the International Conference on Population and Development, the Millennium Summit, the International Conference on Financing for Development, the World Summit on Sustainable Development, the Second World Assembly on Ageing and the twenty-third and twenty-fourth special sessions of the General Assembly;

(c) Give priority to assisting the efforts of developing countries to ensure the full and effective participation of women in deciding and implementing development strategies and integrating gender concerns into national programmes, including by providing adequate resources to operational activities for development in support of the efforts of Governments to ensure full and equal access of women to health care, capital, education, training and technology, as well as full and equal participation in all decision-making.

11. The Commission urged multilateral donors, and invited international financial institutions, within their respective mandates, and regional development banks to review and implement policies to support national efforts to ensure that a higher proportion of resources reached women, in particular in rural and remote areas.

12. The Commission underlined the importance of incorporating a gender, human rights and socio-economic perspective in all policies relevant to education, health and work and to creating an enabling environment for achieving gender equality and the advancement of women, and called upon Governments to:

(*a*) Ensure women's and girls' full and equal access to all levels of quality education and training, while ensuring progressively and on the basis of equal opportunities that primary education was compulsory, accessible and available free to all;

(*b*) Incorporate gender perspectives and human rights in health-sector policies and programmes, pay attention to women's specific needs and priorities, ensure women's right to the highest attainable standards of physical and mental health and their access to affordable and adequate health-care services, including sexual, reproductive and maternal health care and life-saving obstetric care, in accordance with the Programme of Action of the International Conference on Population and Development, and recognize that the lack of economic empowerment and independence increased women's vulnerability to a range of negative consequences, involving the risk of contracting HIV/AIDS, malaria, tuberculosis and other poverty-related diseases;

(*c*) Take all appropriate measures to respond to the concern that the HIV/AIDS pandemic reinforced gender inequalities, that women and girls bore a disproportionate share of the burden imposed by the HIV/AIDS crisis, that they were infected more easily, that they played a key role in care and that they had become more vulnerable to poverty as a result of the HIV/AIDS crisis;

(*d*) Promote respect and realization of the principles contained in the Declaration on Fundamental Principles and Rights at Work and its Follow-up,[93] consider ratification and full implementation of conventions of the International Labour Organization, design policies and programmes that were particularly relevant to providing equal access for women to productive employment and decent work, remove structural and legal barriers, as well as stereotypical attitudes to gender equality at work, promote equal pay for equal work or work of equal value, promote the recognition of the value of women's unremunerated work, and develop and promote policies that facilitated the reconciliation of employment and family responsibilities and access to work for women with disabilities.

---

[93] Adopted on 18 June 1998 by the International Labour Conference at its eighty-sixth session.

Agreed conclusions
Equal participation of women and men in decision-making processes at all levels

1.   The Commission on the Status of Women reaffirmed the Beijing Declaration and Platform for Action, which emphasized that without the active participation of women and the incorporation of women's perspectives at all levels of decision-making, the goals of equality, development and peace could not be achieved, and that women's equal participation was a necessary condition for women's and girls' interests to be taken into account and was needed in order to strengthen democracy and promote its proper functioning.

2.   The Commission reaffirmed the outcome document adopted by the General Assembly at its twenty-third special session,[94] paragraph 23 of which acknowledged that despite general acceptance of the need for gender balance in decision-making bodies at all levels, a gap between de jure and de facto equality had persisted, and that women continued to be under-represented at the legislative, ministerial and sub-ministerial levels, as well as at the highest levels of the corporate sector and other economic and social institutions, and drew attention to the obstacles that hindered women's entry into decision-making positions.

3.   The Commission reaffirmed also the commitment to the equal participation of women and men in public life enshrined in the Universal Declaration of Human Rights and the International Covenant on Civil and Political Rights, and in the Convention on the Political Rights of Women,[95] which stated that women should be on equal terms with men, without any discrimination, entitled to vote in all elections, eligible for election to all publicly elected bodies established by national law, and entitled to hold public office and to exercise all public functions established by national law.

4.   The Commission recalled the Convention on the Elimination of All Forms of Discrimination against Women, which stated, inter alia, that States Parties should take all appropriate measures, including positive measures and temporary special measures, to eliminate discrimination against women and girls in the political and public life of the country.[96]

5.   The Commission urged States parties to comply fully with their obligations under the Convention on the Elimination of All Forms of Dis-

---

[94]   General Assembly resolution S-23/3, annex.

[95]   General Assembly resolutions 217 A (III), 2200 A (XXI), annex, and 640 (VII), annex.

[96]   General Assembly resolution 34/180, annex.

crimination against Women and the Optional Protocol thereto and to take into consideration the concluding comments, as well as the general recommendations of the Committee on the Elimination of Discrimination against Women.[97]

6.   The Commission noted that some States parties had modified their reservations, expressed satisfaction that some reservations had been withdrawn and urged States parties to limit the extent of any reservations that they lodged to the Convention, to formulate any such reservations as precisely and as narrowly as possible, to ensure that no reservations were incompatible with the object and purpose of the Convention, to review their reservations regularly with a view to withdrawing them and to withdraw reservations that were contrary to the object and purpose of the Convention.[98]

7.   The Commission recalled General Assembly resolution 58/142, of 22 December 2003, on women and political participation, in paragraph 1 of which the Assembly urged all stakeholders to develop a comprehensive set of programmes and policies to increase women's participation, especially in political decision-making.

8.   The Commission also recalled that its agreed conclusions 1997/2 on women in power and decision-making recognized the need to accelerate the implementation of strategies that promoted gender balance in political decision-making and to mainstream a gender perspective in all stages of policy formulation and decision-making.

9.   The Commission welcomed the 2005 World Summit, which had reaffirmed that the full and effective implementation of the goals and objectives of the Beijing Declaration and Platform for Action was an essential contribution to achieving the internationally agreed development goals, including the Millennium Development Goals, and had resolved to promote increased representation of women in Government decision-making bodies, including through ensuring their equal opportunity to participate fully in the political process.[99]

10.   The Commission recognized that some progress had been achieved since the Fourth World Conference on Women in women's participation in decision-making at all levels. Introduction of policies and programmes, including positive measures, at the local, national and international levels, had resulted in an increase in women's participation in decision-making processes.

---

[97]   General Assembly resolution 60/230, para. 4.

[98]   Ibid., para. 6.

[99]   General Assembly resolution 60/1, para. 58.

11.	The Commission expressed concern at the serious and persistent obstacles, which were many and varied in nature, that still hindered the advancement of women and further affected their participation in decision-making processes, including, inter alia, the persistent feminization of poverty, the lack of equal access to health, education, training and employment, armed conflict, the lack of security and natural disasters.

12.	The Commission underlined the importance of the empowerment of women and their effective participation in decision-making and policymaking processes as critical tools to prevent and eliminate gender-based violence, and recognized that eliminating all forms of violence against women and girls enabled them to participate equally in decision-making.

13.	The Commission expressed concern about the lack, at the local, national, regional and international levels, of sufficient information and data disaggregated by sex on the participation of women and men in decision-making processes in all areas, including the economy, the public and private sectors, the judiciary, international affairs, academia, trade unions, the media, non-governmental organizations and others.

14.	The Commission reaffirmed the important role of women in the prevention and resolution of conflicts and in peacebuilding, and stressed the importance of their full and equal participation in all efforts to maintain and promote peace and security, and the need to increase their role in decision-making with regard to conflict prevention and resolution and the rebuilding of post-conflict society, in accordance with Security Council resolution 1325 (2000) of 31 October 2000 and the relevant resolutions of the General Assembly.[100]

15.	The Commission recognized that gender equality, development and peace were key issues for the promotion of women, and that new efforts were needed by all actors to create an enabling environment in decision-making.

16.	The Commission reaffirmed the urgent goal of achieving 50/50 gender distribution in all categories of posts within the United Nations system, especially at senior and policymaking levels, with full respect for the principle of equitable geographical distribution, in conformity with Article 101, paragraph 3, of the Charter of the United Nations, and also taking into account the continuing lack of representation or the underrepresentation of women from certain countries, in particular from developing countries, countries with economies in transition, and unrepresented or largely underrepresented Member States.[101]

---

[100]	See General Assembly resolution 58/142, preamble.
[101]	See General Assembly resolution 58/144, para. 3.

17.   The Commission urged Governments, and/or, as appropriate, the relevant entities of the United Nations system, other international and regional organizations, including the international financial institutions, national parliaments, political parties, civil society, including the private sector, trade unions, academia, the media, non-governmental organizations and other actors, to take the following actions:

(*a*)   Ensure that women had the right to vote and exercise that right without duress, persuasion or coercion;

(*b*)   Review, as appropriate, existing legislation, including electoral law, and remove or modify, as appropriate, provisions that hindered women's equal participation in decision-making, and adopt positive actions and temporary special measures, as appropriate, to enhance women's equal participation in decision-making processes at all levels;

(*c*)   Establish concrete goals, targets and benchmarks for achieving equal participation of women and men in decision-making bodies at all levels and in all areas, especially in areas of macroeconomic policy, trade, labour, budgets, defence and foreign affairs, the media and the judiciary, including through positive actions and temporary special measures, as appropriate;

(*d*)   Develop and fund policies and programmes, including innovative measures, to build a critical mass of women leaders, executives and managers, with the goal of achieving a gender balance at all levels and in all areas, in particular in strategic economic, social and political decision-making positions;

(*e*)   Establish the goal of gender balance in decision-making in administration and public appointments at all levels, develop alternative approaches and changes in institutional structures and practices, including gender action plans, which established concrete strategies and budgets for the achievement of consistent gender mainstreaming as a strategy for promoting gender-equality objectives, in legislation and public policies, among others;

(*f*)   Ensure women's full and equal participation and representation at all decision-making levels in all aspects of peace processes and in post-conflict peacebuilding, reconstruction, rehabilitation and reconciliation processes;

(*g*)   Encourage greater involvement of all marginalized women in decision-making at all levels and address and counter the barriers faced by marginalized women in accessing and participating in politics and decision-making;[102]

---

[102]   General Assembly resolution 58/142, para. 1 (*k*).

(*h*) Ensure that gender perspectives were incorporated in development policies and programmes, and in the implementation of the Millennium Development Goals, to ensure that women and all other members of society benefited from development and that women were empowered to assume leadership positions;

(*i*) Promote and strengthen international cooperation to accelerate the development process in which women played a key role and should be equal beneficiaries;

(*j*) Introduce more effective measures aimed at eradicating poverty of women and improving their living conditions to promote the realization of their full human potential, and enable their advancement and their equal participation in decision-making;

(*k*) Ensure that women and girls had equal access to education in all forms and that education was gender-sensitive, and promote educational programmes in which women and girls would be equipped with the necessary knowledge and prepared to participate equally in decision-making processes in all spheres of life and at all levels;

(*l*) Ensure women's and girls' access to training that enabled them to develop their skills, capacities and expertise to exercise leadership, including tools, training and special programmes necessary to enter, inter alia, into politics, including at the highest levels, recognizing existing power differentials in society and the need to respect different positive models of leadership;

(*m*) Ensure women's equal access to decent work, full and productive employment, productive and financial resources and information, in order to facilitate their full and equal participation in decision-making processes at all levels;

(*n*) Introduce objective and transparent procedures for recruitment and gender-sensitive career planning to enable women to assume decision-making positions at all levels and in all areas in order to break the glass ceiling;[103]

(*o*) Eliminate occupational segregation, gender wage gaps, as well as discrimination against women, including marginalized women, in the labour market, through legal and policy measures, including by increasing opportunities for women and girls, as well as men and boys, to work in non-traditional sectors;

(*p*) Ensure women's access to microcredit and microfinance schemes, which had proven to be effective means to empower women and

---

[103] See Commission on the Status of Women, agreed conclusions 1997/3, para. 10.

could create an enabling environment to facilitate their full and equal participation in the decision-making processes at all levels, particularly at the grass-roots level;

(q) Foster an enabling environment in decision-making processes at all levels, including through measures aimed at reconciling family and employment responsibilities, inter alia, by better sharing of paid and unpaid work between women and men;

(r) Take measures to prevent and eliminate all forms of violence against women and girls, in order to promote their full and equal participation in public and political life;

(s) Promote women's leadership in all areas and at all levels and remove all barriers that directly or indirectly hindered the participation of women, in order to increase the visibility and influence of women in decision-making processes;

(t) Facilitate networking and mentoring among women leaders and girls, as appropriate, at all levels and in all areas, including in politics, academia, trade unions, the media and civil society organizations, specifically women's groups and networks, including through the use of information and communication technology, as appropriate;

(u) Encourage, particularly among men and women in decision-making positions, the promotion of gender equality and the empowerment of women, and support women's participation, representation and leadership in decision-making processes at all levels, including the exchange of best practices and awareness-raising;

(v) Develop strategies to increase the involvement of men and boys in promoting gender equality and the empowerment of women, through, inter alia, encouraging the sharing of household work and care;

(w) Develop strategies to eliminate gender stereotypes in all spheres of life, particularly in the media, and foster the positive portrayal of women and girls as leaders and decision makers on all levels and in all areas;

(x) Recognize the importance of women's participation in decision-making in all areas, including the political process, provide fair and balanced coverage of male and female candidates, cover participation in women's political organizations and ensure coverage of issues that had a particular impact on women;[104]

---

[104] General Assembly resolution 58/142, para. 2 (*m*).

(y) Adopt clear rules, as necessary, for candidate selection within parties, including, as appropriate, the implementation of concrete goals, targets and benchmarks, including, where appropriate, temporary special measures, such as quotas, for achieving equitable representation of women candidates in elected positions;

(z) Promote women's candidacies in elections, inter alia and as appropriate, through the adoption of specific measures, such as training programmes and recruitment drives and, as a temporary special measure, consider funding for women candidates;

(aa) Make efforts to ensure equal opportunities during election campaigns, including equal access to the media and to financial and other resources, as appropriate;

(bb) Facilitate the inclusion of women in decision-making positions within electoral management bodies and observer commissions and give consideration to gender equality and the empowerment of women in the structure and activities of such bodies;

(cc) Consider establishing parliamentary standing or ad hoc committees or other statutory bodies on gender equality and empowerment of women, with cross-party representation, where appropriate, to monitor and review the implementation of existing laws and constitutional provisions, in line with the Convention on the Elimination of All Forms of Discrimination against Women, where applicable, and the commitments to implement the Beijing Platform for Action and the outcome document of the twenty-third special session of the General Assembly, as well as taking into account recommendations of the Committee on the Elimination of All Forms of Discrimination against Women, where applicable;

(dd) Consider ratifying and implementing relevant instruments relating to full political, economic, social and cultural rights for women and girls, especially the Convention on the Elimination of All Forms of Discrimination against Women, the International Covenant on Civil and Political Rights, the International Covenant on Economic, Social and Cultural Rights, and the Convention on the Rights of the Child;

(ee) Reaffirm the Universal Declaration of Human Rights as a vital instrument for the advancement of women and, in that regard, take measures to achieve the Millennium Development Goals and other internationally agreed development goals;

(ff) Encourage public dissemination of national periodic reports to the Committee on the Elimination of All Forms of Discrimination against Women, as well as concluding comments provided by the Committee;

(gg) Promote collaboration among all relevant actors, such as parliaments, national machineries for the advancement of women and other relevant national mechanisms, and women's groups and networks in civil society to advance gender equality and the empowerment of women;

(hh) Support the mainstreaming of a gender perspective at all levels and stages of the budgetary process, including through awareness-raising and training, where appropriate;

(ii) Strengthen research, monitoring and evaluation of the progress of women's participation in decision-making at all levels, in particular in areas where there was a dearth of information, including, as appropriate, through the development of acceptable standardized methodology for systematic collection of gender-specific data and statistics, disaggregated by sex and other relevant factors, and disseminate lessons learned and good practices;

(jj) Ensure political will to recognize the role of women in development in all spheres of life, to promote gender equality and favour the participation of women in decision-making positions.

Fifty-first session
26 February–9 March 2007

Agreed conclusions:

Elimination of all forms of discrimination and violence against the girl child

The agreed conclusions adopted for the fifty-first session of the Commission on the Status of Women can be found in the *Official Records of the Economic and Social Council, 2007, Supplement No. 7* (E/2007/27-E/CN.6/2007/9).

Agreed conclusions

Elimination of all forms of discrimination and violence against the girl child

1.   The Commission on the Status of Women reaffirms the Beijing Declaration and Platform for Action, the outcome documents of the twenty-third special session of the General Assembly and the declaration adopted by the Commission on the occasion of the tenth anniversary of the Fourth World Conference on Women.

2.   The Commission also reaffirms the outcome of the 2002 World Summit on Children and the international commitments to gender equality and the elimination of all forms of discrimination and violence against the girl child made at the World Conference on Human Rights, the International Conference on Population and Development, the World Summit for Social Development and the World Conference against Racism, Racial Discrimination, Xenophobia and Related Intolerance, as well as those made in the United Nations Millennium Declaration and at the 2005 World Summit, and reaffirms further that their full and effective and accelerated implementation are integral to achieving the internationally agreed development goals, including the Millennium Development Goals.

3.   The Commission reiterates that the Convention on the Elimination of All Forms of Discrimination against Women and its Optional Protocol and the Convention on the Rights of the Child and its Optional Protocols, as well as other conventions and treaties, provide a legal framework and a comprehensive set of measures for the promotion and protection of the human rights of the girl child, including for the elimination of all forms of discrimination and violence against her. In this regard, the Commission welcomes the adoption in December 2006 of the Convention on the Rights of Persons with Disabilities.

4.   The Commission reaffirms the commitment to the full and effective implementation of, and follow-up to, all relevant resolutions of the General Assembly and of the Economic and Social Council and its subsidiary bodies on the girl child, its previous set of agreed conclusions on the girl child, as well as Security Council resolutions 1325 and 1612.

5.   The Commission welcomes the June 2006 Political Declaration on HIV/AIDS, which expressed grave concern for the overall expansion and feminization of the HIV pandemic and recognized that gender inequalities and all forms of violence against women and girls increased their vulnerability to HIV/AIDS.

6.   The Commission reaffirms the commitment to ensure the full implementation of the human rights of women and of the girl child as an

inalienable, integral and indivisible part of all human rights and fundamental freedoms.

7.   The Commission is profoundly concerned that previous goals and targets and commitments, including financial commitments, made with regard to the girl child remain unfulfilled and that, despite progress in addressing all forms of discrimination and violence against girls and recognition of their rights, discrimination and violations of their human rights still persist.

8.   The Commission recognizes that the empowerment of girls is key to breaking the cycle of discrimination and violence and to promoting and protecting the full and effective enjoyment of all their human rights. It also recognizes that empowering girls requires the active support and engagement of their parents, legal guardians, families, boys and men, as well as the wider community.

9.   The Commission also recognizes that the difficult socio-economic conditions that exist in many developing countries, particularly the least developed countries, have resulted in the acceleration of the feminization of poverty and that in situations of poverty girl children are among those most affected. In this regard, the Commission stresses that achieving the Millennium Development Goals by 2015 and all other agreed development goals is a global effort and an essential element in improving the situation of girl children and ensuring their human rights. The Commission further recognizes that, as part of urgent national and international action required to eradicate poverty, investing in the development of girls is a priority in and of itself and has a multiplier effect, in particular on productivity, efficiency and sustained economic growth.

10.   The Commission expresses concern that the girl child does not receive sufficiently explicit attention in policy and programme development and resource allocation. It is also concerned that the lack of resources and data disaggregated by sex, age and other relevant factors addressing the specific situation of vulnerable girls remains a serious constraint in formulating and implementing effective, targeted policies and programmes and monitoring progress in eliminating all forms of discrimination and violence.

11.   The Commission notes with appreciation the United Nations study on violence against children and the Secretary-General's in-depth study on violence against women and takes into account their recommendations.

12.   The Commission recognizes that prevailing negative sociocultural attitudes and gender stereotypes contribute to the de facto and de jure discrimination against the girl child and violations of the rights of the girl child.

13. The Commission urges Governments to take the following actions:

Norms and policies

(a) Consider ratifying or acceding to, as a particular matter of priority, the Convention on the Rights of the Child and the Convention on the Elimination of All Forms of Discrimination against Women and their respective Optional Protocols, limit the extent of any reservations that they lodge and regularly review such reservations with a view to withdrawing them so as to ensure that no reservation is incompatible with the object and purpose of the relevant treaty; and implement them fully by, inter alia, putting in place effective national legislation, policies and action plans;

(b) Consider ratifying or acceding to, as a matter of priority, the United Nations Convention against Transnational Organized Crime and the Protocols thereto, in particular the Protocol to Prevent, Suppress and Punish Trafficking in Persons, Especially Women and Children;

(c) Consider becoming a State Party to, as a matter of priority, and thereafter ensure the full implementation of, International Labour Organization (ILO) Conventions 138 and 182 on, respectively, the minimum age for employment, and eliminating the worst forms of child labour, and establish appropriate penalties and sanctions to ensure effective enforcement;

(d) Intensify efforts to fully implement the Beijing Platform for Action, the outcome documents of the five-year review of the Beijing Platform for Action, the World Summit for Children and the Millennium Development Goals;

(e) Exercise leadership to end all forms of violence against girls and support advocacy in this regard at all levels, including at the local, national, regional and international levels, and by all sectors, especially by political, community and religious leaders, as well as the public and private sectors, the media and civil society;

(f) Review and, where appropriate, revise, amend or abolish all laws, regulations, policies, practices and customs that discriminate against women or the girl child or have a discriminatory impact on women or the girl child, and ensure that provisions of multiple legal systems, where they exist, comply with international human rights obligations, commitments and principles, including the principle of non-discrimination;

(g) Condemn all forms of discrimination and violence against girls and enact and/or strengthen legislation on preventing and eliminating all forms of discrimination and violence against girls, develop policies that ensure its full and effective implementation, and put in place adequate national and local mechanisms to monitor compliance with these laws and policies, with the active participation of civil society, where appropriate;

(*h*) Develop policies and programmes to sensitize magistrates, judges, lawyers, prosecutors and persons who work with victims, in order to ensure that judicial proceedings are adequate to the needs and the development of the girl child and that a gender perspective is applied to such proceedings;

(*i*) Exercise due diligence to prevent all forms of violence against girls, and investigate and punish the perpetrators of such violence and provide protection to the victims;

(*j*) Create, where not currently in place, and maintain birth, death and marriage data registries with full national coverage;

(*k*) Review, enact and strictly enforce laws and regulations concerning the minimum legal age of consent and the minimum age for marriage, raising the minimum age for marriage where necessary, and generate social support for the enforcement of these laws, inter alia, through increasing educational opportunities for girls and advocating the benefits of keeping girls in schools;

(*l*) Give explicit attention to the girl child in budget processes at all levels, including resource allocation and expenditure reviews, to ensure the mobilization of sufficient resources for the elimination of all forms of discrimination and violence against girls.

14.   The Commission, taking into account the primary responsibility of Governments in the fight against all forms of discrimination, exploitation and violence against the girl child, urges Governments and/or the relevant funds and programmes, organs and specialized agencies of the United Nations system, within their respective mandates, and invites the international financial institutions and all relevant actors of civil society, including non-governmental organizations and the private sector, to:

14.1.   *Poverty*

(*a*) Reduce social and economic inequalities, giving priority to approaches that focus on poverty eradication and improving linkages, participation and social networks within and between different community groups, thereby addressing economic, social and cultural rights and reducing the vulnerability of the girl child to discrimination and violence;

(*b*) Integrate a gender perspective, giving explicit attention to the girl child, in national development strategies, plans and policies, and provide support to developing countries in the implementation of these development strategies, policies and plans;

(*c*) Improve the situation of girl children living in poverty, deprived of nutrition, water and sanitation facilities, with no access to basic health-care services, shelter, education, participation and protection, taking into account that while a severe lack of goods and services hurts every human being, it is most threatening and harmful to the girl child, leaving her unable to enjoy her rights, to reach her full potential and to participate as a full member of society;

(*d*) Assess the impact of globalization, economic policies and the constraints of the international trade system on the girl child and mainstream a gender perspective, giving explicit attention to the girl child, into all development policies and programmes and poverty eradication strategies, where appropriate;

14.2. *Education and training*

(*a*) Intensify their efforts to meet the target of eliminating gender inequalities in primary and secondary education by the earliest possible date and at all educational levels by 2015, including through the provision of Education for All partnerships;

(*b*) Collect data disaggregated by sex and age on dropout rates at all levels of education, and conduct research on the causes, including root causes, of the discontinuation of education by girls;

(*c*) Ensure that all children, particularly girls, without discrimination on the basis of race, ethnicity or disability, have equal access to, and complete, free and compulsory primary education of good quality, and renew their efforts to improve and expand girls' education at all levels, including the secondary and higher levels, in all academic areas, as well as vocational education and technical training, in order to, inter alia, encourage women to enter the labour market and as a way of achieving gender equality, the empowerment of women and poverty eradication, and to allow women's full and equal contribution to, and equal opportunity to benefit from, development;

(*d*) Recognize the critical role of both formal and non-formal education in the achievement of poverty eradication and other development goals, including the Millennium Development Goals, and ensure access of women and girls to non-formal education, particularly for those who are dropouts and living in poverty, with the aim to equip them with the necessary knowledge and prepare them to participate equally in decision-making in all spheres of life and at all levels;

(e) Identify constraints and gaps and develop appropriate strategies, in collaboration with parents and legal guardians, teachers and community leaders, to ensure gender equality, accelerated achievement of equality in enrolment and completion of schooling at the early childhood, primary and all other educational levels for all girls, including pregnant adolescents and young mothers, especially in neglected and marginalized areas and communities and rural and remote areas, and introduce, where appropriate, temporary special measures, including financial incentives and stipends and nutrition programmes in order to improve enrolment and retention rates for girls at all educational levels;

(f) Promote gender-sensitive, empowering educational and training processes and teaching materials by, inter alia, reviewing and revising, as appropriate, school curricula, formal and non-formal educational and training materials and teacher-training programmes, including for those dealing with career orientation, and encourage and support girls' and boys' interest and involvement in non-traditional fields and occupations;

(g) Ensure safe and supportive school environments for girls and girl-friendly school premises by implementing measures to eliminate discrimination and violence against girls and specific measures against sexual harassment at school, achieving gender balance at all levels in the education sector, providing appropriate sanitation and recreational facilities, boarding facilities, and school transport, where appropriate, and securing safe routes to and from school;

(h) Develop well-resourced educational and livelihood-skills programmes to reach girls who are not enrolled in formal education programmes owing to specific life circumstances, inter alia, extreme poverty, child labour, abuse or exploitation, trafficking, prostitution, armed conflict and displacement, migration, early and forced marriage, pregnancy, motherhood and disability;

(i) Ensure girls' access to training that enables them to develop their skills, capacities and expertise to exercise leadership, including tools, training and special programmes necessary to become actors in public life, including at the highest levels, addressing existing power differentials in society and the need for different positive models of leadership;

(j) Ensure that young women and men have access to information and education, including peer education, youth-specific HIV education and sexual education and services necessary for behavioural change, to develop the life skills required to reduce their vulnerability to HIV infection and reproductive ill health, in full partnership with young persons, parents, families, educators and health-care providers;

(*k*) Ensure that the rights of the girl child are fully integrated into all peace and non-violence education, including on peacemaking, peacekeeping and peacebuilding, which should be provided from the primary level on as a means of instructing girls and boys in the prevention, resolution and management of conflicts at the inter-personal, community, national and international levels;

(*l*) Increase girls' ability to attend school and extra-curricular activi-ties by investing in public infrastructure projects and quality public services, such as transport, water, sanitation and sustain-able energy, in order to reduce the amount of time girls spend on everyday routine household maintenance tasks, while also work-ing to change attitudes that reinforce the division of labour based on gender, in order to promote shared family responsibility for work in the home and reduce the domestic work burden for girls;

(*m*) Promote and support increased access of girls to information and communications technology (ICT), particularly girls living in poverty, girls living in rural and remote areas and in disadvan-taged situations, and enhance international support to overcome the digital divide among countries and regions, between men and women and boys and girls, as well as between different social groups of women and girls;

(*n*) Create literate environments and societies, eradicating illiteracy among women and girls and eliminating the gender gap in lit-eracy, inter alia, by intensifying efforts to implement effectively the International Plan of Action for the United Nations Literacy Decade and integrating substantially those efforts in the Educa-tion for All process and other activities of the United Nations Educational, Scientific and Cultural Organization (UNESCO), as well as other literacy initiatives within the framework of the inter-nationally agreed development goals, including the Millennium Development Goals;

(*o*) Allocate sufficient resources and provide technical assistance upon request to developing countries in order to strengthen the capac-ity to provide equal access to education and to monitor progress in closing the gap between girls and boys in education, training and research, and in levels of achievement in all fields, particularly basic education and literacy programmes;

14.3. *Gender stereotypes*

(*a*) Recognize that eliminating stereotypes calls for a deep societal change that needs to be supported through the development of strategies to eliminate gender stereotypes in all spheres of life, and foster the positive portrayal of women and girls at all levels, including as leaders and decision makers, including through developing and implementing appropriate legislation, policies and programmes, as well as awareness campaigns, to address stereotypical attitudes and behaviours that contribute to discrimination and violence against girls;

(b) Target and work with men and boys, as well as women and girls and other actors, such as parents, teachers, religious and traditional leaders and educational and media institutions, to address stereotypical attitudes and behaviours, and encourage decision makers at all levels with responsibilities for policies, legislation, programmes and allocation of public resources to play leadership roles in the elimination of all forms of discrimination and violence against girls and in the promotion of girls empowerment;

(c) Ensure that men and women, and boys and girls are educated on girls' rights and their responsibility to respect the rights of others, inter alia, by integrating girls' rights into appropriate curricula at all levels, including in schools and the vocational training of health workers, teachers, law enforcement personnel, military personnel, social workers, the judiciary, community leaders, the media and others and encourage men and boys to speak out strongly against all forms of discrimination and violence against women and girls and not to protect perpetrators or condone their violence;

(d) Promote non-discriminatory treatment of girls and boys in the family and, in this regard, adopt measures to ensure equal access by girls and boys to food, education and health, and develop programmes and policies addressed to family members, especially parents and other legal guardians, to protect and promote the health and well-being of girls, as well as to ensure that the value of girls to their families and societies is recognized, including with a view to eliminating son preference;

(e) Encourage cooperation and dialogue between Governments and all relevant actors so that media contents, including the portrayal of gender stereotypes, prejudices and violence, are reviewed, consistent with freedom of expression, and that the quality of programmes broadcast can be improved;

(f) Encourage the active participation of boys, from an early age, in the elimination of discrimination and violence against girls, including through the promotion of gender-sensitive socialization processes, targeted programmes and creation of spaces and environments where boys and girls can be guided in challenging gender stereotypes and negative attitudes towards girls;

14.4. *Health*

(a) Take all necessary measures to ensure the rights of girls to the enjoyment of the highest attainable standard of health, and develop sustainable health systems and social services, ensuring access to such systems and services without discrimination, paying special attention to adequate food and nutrition and the effects of communicable diseases and to the special needs of adolescents, including raising awareness about eating disorders, and to sexual and reproductive health, and securing appropriate prenatal and post-natal care, including measures to prevent mother-to-child transmission of HIV;

(b) Ensure the availability of and access to comprehensive age-appropriate information, education and confidential counselling for girls and boys, including in school curricula, on human relationships, and sexual and reproductive health, sexually transmitted infections, including HIV/AIDS, and the prevention of early pregnancy, that emphasize the equal rights and responsibility of girls and boys;

(c) Develop, implement and support national and international prevention, care and treatment strategies, as appropriate, to effectively address the condition of obstetric fistula and to further develop a multisectoral, multidisciplinary, comprehensive and integrated approach in order to bring about lasting solutions and put an end to obstetric fistula, maternal mortality and related morbidities, including through ensuring access to affordable, comprehensive, quality maternal health-care services, including skilled birth attendance and emergency obstetric care;

(d) Develop and implement national legislation and policies prohibiting harmful customary or traditional practices, particularly female genital mutilation, that are violations of and obstacles to the full enjoyment by women of their human rights and fundamental freedoms, and prosecute the perpetrators of such practices that are harmful to the health of women and girls;

14.5. *HIV/AIDS*

(a) Ensure that in all policies and programmes designed to provide comprehensive HIV/AIDS prevention, treatment, care and support, particular attention and support is given to the girl child at risk, infected with, and affected by HIV/AIDS, including pregnant girls and young and adolescent mothers, as part of the global effort to scale up significantly towards the goal of universal access to comprehensive prevention, treatment, care and support by 2010;

(*b*) Provide appropriate information to help young women, including adolescent girls, understand their sexuality, including their sexual and reproductive health, in order to increase their ability to protect themselves from HIV infection and sexually transmitted infections and unwanted pregnancy;

(*c*) Educate men and boys to accept their role and responsibility in the spreading of HIV/AIDS and in matters related to sexuality, reproduction and child-rearing and to promote equality between women and men, girls and boys;

(*d*) Address the underlying and root causes of the feminization of HIV/AIDS, and take appropriate measures to provide a supportive and socially inclusive environment for girls infected with, and affected by, HIV/AIDS, including by providing appropriate counselling and psychosocial support, ensuring their enrolment in school and equal access to shelter, nutrition, health and social services and taking effective measures to eliminate stigmatization, discrimination, violence, exploitation and abuse on the basis of HIV or AIDS status;

(*e*) Identify and address the needs of girls heading households, including in the context of the HIV/AIDS pandemic, for, inter alia, protection, access to financial resources, access to health care and support services, including affordable HIV/AIDS treatment, and for opportunities to continue their education, with particular attention to orphans and vulnerable children, and increase men's responsibility for home-based care in order to address the disproportionate burden borne by women and girls in caring for the chronically ill;

(*f*) Increase global efforts to overcome any legal, regulatory, trade and other barriers that block access to prevention, treatment, care and support, and allocate adequate resources;

(*g*) Promote initiatives aimed at reducing the prices of antiretroviral drugs, especially second-line drugs, available to the girl child, including bilateral and private sector initiatives, as well as initiatives on a voluntary basis by groups of States, based on innovative financing mechanisms that contribute to the mobilization of resources for social development, including those that aim to provide further access to drugs at affordable prices to developing countries on a sustainable and predictable basis, and in this regard take note of the International Drug Purchase Facility;

14.6.   *Child labour*

(*a*) Ensure that the applicable ILO requirements for the employment of girls and boys are respected and effectively enforced, and ensure also that girls who are employed have equal access to decent work, equal payment and remuneration and are protected from economic exploitation, discrimination, sexual harassment, violence and abuse in the workplace, are aware of their rights, and have access to formal and non-formal education, skills development, and vocational training, and develop gender-sensitive measures, including national action plans where appropriate, to eliminate the worst forms of child labour, including commercial sexual exploitation, slave-like practices, forced and bonded labour, trafficking, and hazardous forms of child labour;

(b) Raise government and public awareness as to the nature and scope of the special needs of girls, including migrant girls, employed as domestic workers and of those performing excessive domestic chores in their own households, and develop measures to prevent their labour and economic exploitation and sexual abuse, and ensure that they have access to education and vocational training, health services, food, shelter and recreation;

14.7. *Armed conflict*

(a) Take special measures for the protection of girls affected by armed conflict and by post-conflict situations and, in particular, protect them from sexually transmitted diseases, such as HIV/AIDS, gender-based violence, including rape and sexual abuse, and sexual exploitation, torture, abduction and forced labour, paying special attention to refugee and displaced girls; and take into account the special needs of girls affected by unilateral measures not in accordance with international law and the Charter of the United Nations and by armed conflicts in the delivery of humanitarian assistance and disarmament, demobilization, rehabilitation assistance and reintegration processes, and that girls living under foreign occupation must also be protected in accordance with the provisions of international humanitarian law;

(b) Incorporate a gender perspective, including special attention to the girl child, in the mandates, operational guidelines and training programmes of peacekeeping forces, police, humanitarian workers and associated civilian personnel in armed conflict and post-conflict situations;

(c) Take appropriate measures to ensure that the specific needs of girls are addressed in all aspects of preventing the recruitment of children in armed groups and armed forces, and to facilitate their release and reintegration and secure the effective access of girls to dedicated programmes and services that respond to their specific needs for protection and assistance, and develop strategies to prevent future stigmatization and discrimination in their community and family and, in this regard, elaborate and implement applicable operational policies and frameworks based on good practices and lessons learned;

(*d*) Ensure that sufficient attention is given to the girl child in all frameworks and action plans addressing violations and abuses against children in armed conflict;

14.8. *Humanitarian assistance to girls*

Take measures to ensure that the specific needs of girls affected by armed conflict and natural disasters are taken into account in the delivery of humanitarian assistance and finding durable solutions, including in refugee camps and camps for the internally displaced and in reconstruction efforts, and ensure that such assistance is provided in full compliance with international law, and in accordance with General Assembly resolution 46/182 in the context of United Nations humanitarian assistance;

14.9. *Violence and discrimination*

(*a*) Condemn all forms of violence against girls and take effective legislative and other measures to prevent and eliminate all such violence, including physical, mental, psychological and sexual violence, torture, child abuse and exploitation, hostage-taking, domestic violence, trafficking in or sale of children and their organs, paedophilia, child prostitution, child pornography, child sex tourism, gang-related violence and harmful traditional practices in all settings;

(*b*) Take all appropriate measures to strengthen legal frameworks, including the review and amendment of existing legislation, the enactment of new laws where necessary, developing adequate programmes and formulating appropriate policies to prevent, prosecute and punish all cases of violence against girls, including threats of such acts, coercion or arbitrary deprivation of liberty, whether occurring in public or private life, and in particular physical, sexual, and psychological violence, wherever it occurs, within or outside the family;

(*c*) Provide age-appropriate and gender-sensitive services to girls subjected to all forms of gender-based violence, including comprehensive programmes for their physical, psychological and social recovery, such as health, counselling and legal services, helplines and shelters, and ensure adequate human, material and financial resources for these services;

(*d*) Condemn violence against women and girls and refrain from invoking any custom, tradition or religious consideration to avoid their obligations with respect to its elimination, and hold up to public scrutiny and eliminate those attitudes that foster, justify, or tolerate violence;

(e) Strengthen advocacy and rights-based awareness-raising programmes directed at eliminating all forms of violence and discrimination against girls by engaging girls and boys, parents and families, local community, political, religious and traditional leaders and educational institutions, and provide adequate financial support to efforts at both national and local levels to change behaviour, stereotyped attitudes and harmful practices;

(f) Create and support, as appropriate, community-based networks to advocate against all forms of violence against girls, develop programmes to sensitize and train health workers and other professionals working with and for the girl child to the issue, including on the early detection of violence, and integrate comprehensive measures and incentives that promote the full enjoyment of human rights and equality by the girl child into national development strategies;

(g) Encourage and support men and boys to take an active part in the prevention and elimination of all forms of violence, and encourage increased understanding among men and boys of how violence harms girls, boys, women and men and undermines gender equality;

(h) Eliminate all forms of discrimination against the girl child and the root causes of son preference, which results in harmful and unethical practices regarding female infanticide and prenatal sex selection, which may have significant repercussions on society as a whole;

(i) Review, strengthen or adopt legislation or policies to eradicate child pornography, including child pornography transmitted through the media and ICTs, and related forms of exploitation of children, and strengthen efforts to combat the existence of a market that encourages child pornography, including the prosecution of those who sexually exploit or abuse children;

(j) Develop and strengthen partnerships involving Governments, civil society, the media and business sectors and other relevant actors in the elimination of child pornography, including child pornography transmitted through the media and ICTs, in the protection of the girl child from related abuses and exploitation, and in training, inter alia, law enforcers, prosecutors, judges and social workers, as appropriate, in order to build effective capacities to eradicate child pornography;

(k) Ensure that follow-up to and implementation of relevant resolutions and, where appropriate, the relevant recommendations contained in the United Nations study on violence against children and the in-depth study on all forms of violence against women include explicit attention to girls at all levels;

(l) Increase education and training among teachers and health-service providers in identifying acts of violence against the girl child, and ensure that they also take action to eradicate all forms of violence against the girl child, including customary and traditional practices that are harmful to the health of the girl child;

(m) Take measures to protect girls in juvenile detention facilities from all forms of physical, psychological or sexual violence and abuse and ensure that the detention or incarceration of girls shall be used only as a measure of last resort and for the shortest appropriate period of time;

14.10.   *Trafficking*

(a) Take appropriate measures to ensure that all efforts aimed at combating trafficking in persons are gender- and child-sensitive, including in actions to address the factors that increase vulnerability to being trafficked, such as poverty and gender inequality, and to eliminate the demand that fosters all forms of exploitation of women and girls that leads to trafficking, and where girls are identified in situations of exploitation take all appropriate measures to remove them from harm and protect them without delay;

(b) Strengthen and improve international cooperation and coordination, including regional efforts in the fight against trafficking in persons, especially women and girls, in order to prevent trafficking; protect, assist, rehabilitate and reintegrate victims; and prosecute and punish offenders in accordance with due process of law on the basis of the principles of shared responsibility, respect for human rights and the active cooperation of countries of origin, transit and destination and other relevant actors thereto;

14.11.   *Girls in high-risk situations*

Actively support girls vulnerable to all forms of discrimination and violence, including through the allocation of appropriate financial resources and targeted, innovative programmes that address the needs and priorities of girls in high-risk situations who have difficulties accessing services and programmes;

14.12.   *Migration*

(a) Build awareness of the risks encountered by girls in the context of migration, particularly in the context of irregular migration, such as sexual and labour exploitation, migrant smuggling and trafficking in persons, and develop gender-sensitive migration policies and training programmes for law enforcement personnel, prosecutors and service providers that ensure the delivery of proper and professional interventions for girl migrants who are subjected to abuse and violence;

(*b*) Effectively promote and protect the human rights and fundamental freedoms of girl migrants, regardless of their immigration status, and facilitate family reunification in an expeditious and effective manner, with due regard for applicable laws;

14.13. *Empowering girls*

(*a*) Promote people-centred sustainable development, including sustained economic growth, through the provision of basic education, lifelong education, literacy and training, and health care for all girls and women, and assist girls to secure economic independence, particularly girls heading households;

(*b*) Facilitate girls' empowerment, including through developing and adequately funding safe and supportive spaces, promoting mentoring and networking among women leaders and girls at all levels, peer education programmes, life skills programmes, and other gender-sensitive youth-friendly services, and provide enhanced opportunities for girls, particularly adolescent girls, to meet and interact with their peers and develop leadership capacities and networking opportunities;

(*c*) Invest in awareness campaigns, and provide education and training, including specialized training on violence, gender issues, discrimination and human rights, to parents and legal guardians, families, political, religious, traditional and community leaders, and all professions relevant to the protection and empowerment of girls, including educators, social workers, police officers, judges, lawyers, prosecutors and the media, to increase awareness and commitment to the promotion and protection of the rights of girls and appropriate responses to rights violations;

14.14. *Participation of girls*

(*a*) Respect and promote the right of girls to express themselves freely and to take the views of girls into account in all matters affecting them, including by taking all necessary actions to empower girls to exercise this right, according to their evolving capacity, and to build self-esteem and acquire knowledge and skills and provide them with adequate information on health, social and education services, programmes and initiatives to facilitate their participation in all sectors, including civil society;

(*b*) Involve girls, including girls with special needs, and their representative organizations, in decision-making processes, as appropriate, and include them as full and active partners in identifying their own needs and in developing, planning, implementing and assessing policies and programmes to meet these needs;

14.15.   *Gender mainstreaming*

Mainstream a gender perspective, including special attention to the girl child, into all legislation, policies and programmes, and strengthen national monitoring and evaluation, inter alia, by utilizing gender budgeting and gender impact assessment, and compile and disseminate lessons learned and good practices;

14.16.   *Data collection*

(*a*) Encourage and strengthen national research, monitoring and evaluation of the progress in eliminating all forms of discrimination and violence against the girl child, in particular in areas where there is a dearth of information, including, as appropriate, through the development of reliable standardized methodology for the systematic collection, analysis and use in policy formulation of gender-specific data and statistics, disaggregated by sex, age and other relevant factors addressing the specific situation of vulnerable girls, and disseminate lessons learned and good practices;

(*b*) Conduct regular surveys of the situation and needs of girls at national and local levels to identify groups at high risk of discrimination and violence, ensuring that all data are disaggregated by age, education, marital status, geographical location, income and other relevant factors;

(*c*) Collect data disaggregated by age, sex and other relevant factors addressing the specific situation of vulnerable girls and systematically report on internationally agreed indicators related to the girl child as contained in the Millennium Development Goals, and support the development of additional indicators in consultation with the Statistical Commission, as appropriate, to more systematically and effectively measure national progress in eliminating all forms of discrimination and violence against the girl child.

Treaty bodies

15.   The Commission encourages the Committee on the Rights of the Child and the Committee on the Elimination of Discrimination against Women, as well as the other human rights treaty bodies, to invite States parties to ensure that their reports explicitly address the situation of the girl child.

Implementation of commitments

16. · The Commission calls on all States and the international community, including the United Nations system, and invites international and non-governmental organizations and the private sector to mobilize and allocate all necessary resources, support and efforts, including at the international level, to realize the goals, strategic objectives and actions set out in the Beijing Platform for Action with regard to the elimination of all forms of discrimination and violence against the girl child and the further actions and initiatives to implement the Beijing Declaration and Platform for Action, as well as other relevant commitments.

17. The Commission reaffirms the commitment to adequate financial resources at the international level for the implementation of the Beijing Platform for Action, the Cairo Plan of Action and the Beijing+5 outcome document in developing countries, especially through the strengthening of their national capacities.

Support to the United Nations system

18. The Commission calls upon all organizations of the United Nations system, within their organizational mandates, to mainstream a gender perspective and to pursue gender equality in their country programmes, planning instruments and sector-wide programmes, and to articulate specific country-level goals and targets in this field, in accordance with national development strategies.

19. The Commission calls on all States, and invites multilateral, financial and development institutions to support the entities of the United Nations system, especially its funds and programmes, to increase their efforts, including through, as appropriate, the United Nations country teams, to strengthen their country-level advocacy and their technical capacities to address all forms of discrimination and violence against the girl child.

Fifty-second session
25 February–7 and 13 March 2008

Agreed conclusions:

Financing for gender equality and the empowerment of women

The agreed conclusions adopted for the fifty-second session of the Commission on the Status of Women can be found in the *Official Records of the Economic and Social Council, 2008, Supplement No. 7*, (E/2008/27-E/CN.6/2008/11).

Agreed conclusions
Financing for gender equality and the empowerment of women

1. The Commission on the Status of Women reaffirms the Beijing Declaration and Platform for Action, which emphasized the need for political commitment to make available human and financial resources for the empowerment of women and that funding had to be identified and mobilized from all sources and across all sectors to achieve the goals of gender equality and the empowerment of women, and the outcome of the twenty-third special session of the General Assembly, which called upon Governments to incorporate a gender perspective into the design, development, adoption and execution of all policies and budgetary processes, as appropriate, in order to promote equitable, effective and appropriate resource allocation and establish adequate budgetary allocations to support gender equality and development programmes that enhance women's empowerment.

2. The Commission reaffirms the declaration adopted on the occasion of the tenth anniversary of the Fourth World Conference on Women, which stressed that challenges and obstacles remained in the implementation of the Beijing Declaration and Platform for Action and the outcome documents of the twenty-third special session of the General Assembly, and pledged to take further action to ensure their full and accelerated implementation.

3. The Commission recalls the outcome of the International Conference on Financing for Development held in Monterrey, Mexico, in 2002, which affirms, inter alia, that a holistic approach to the interconnected national, international and systemic challenges of financing for development, sustainable, gender-sensitive, people-centred development, in all parts of the globe is essential.

4. The Commission also recalls the 2005 World Summit and reaffirms that the full and effective implementation of the Beijing Declaration and Platform for Action and the outcome of the twenty-third special session of the General Assembly, the International Conference on Population and Development and other relevant United Nations summits and conferences are essential contributions to the achievement of the internationally agreed development goals, including those contained in the United Nations Millennium Declaration, in particular, on the promotion of gender equality and the empowerment of women.

5. The Commission reaffirms the Convention on the Elimination of All Forms of Discrimination against Women and its Optional Protocol and the Convention on the Rights of the Child, and takes note of the work of the

Committee on the Elimination of Discrimination against Women towards the practical realization of the principle of equality between women and men and between girls and boys.

6.   The Commission also reaffirms that States have primary responsibility for promoting gender equality and the empowerment of women and girls and that gender mainstreaming and national machineries are necessary and play a critical role in the implementation of the Beijing Declaration and Platform for Action and that, in order for national machineries to be effective, a strong institutional framework with clear mandates, location at the highest possible level, accountability mechanisms, partnership with civil society, a transparent political process, adequate financial and human resources and continued strong political commitment are crucial.

7.   The Commission recalls that the Platform for Action recognizes that its implementation requires adequate financial resources committed at the national and international levels and that strengthening national capacities in developing countries in this regard requires striving for the fulfilment of the agreed targets of overall official development assistance from developed countries as soon as possible. The Commission recognizes the importance of the full utilization of all sources of development finance.

8.   The Commission also recognizes the importance of gender mainstreaming as a tool for achieving gender equality and, to that end, the need to promote the mainstreaming of a gender perspective in the design, implementation, monitoring and evaluation of policies and programmes in all political, economic and social spheres and to strengthen the capabilities of the United Nations system in the area of gender.

9.   The Commission reaffirms that gender equality and the promotion and protection of the full enjoyment of human rights and fundamental freedoms for all are essential for advancing development, peace and security, and stresses that peace is inextricably linked to equality between women and men and to development.

10.   The Commission reaffirms that the promotion and protection of, and respect for, the human rights and fundamental freedoms of women, including the right to development, which are universal, indivisible, interdependent and interrelated, should be mainstreamed into all policies and programmes aimed at the eradication of poverty, and also reaffirms the need to take measures to ensure that every person is entitled to participate in, contribute to and enjoy economic, social, cultural and political development.

11.   The Commission notes the growing body of evidence demonstrating that investing in women and girls has a multiplier effect on productivity, efficiency and sustained economic growth and that increasing women's economic empowerment is central to the achievement of the Mil-

lennium Development Goals and to the eradication of poverty, and recognizes that adequate resources need to be allocated at all levels, mechanisms and capacities need to be strengthened and gender-responsive policies need to be enhanced to fully utilize the multiplier effect.

12.　The Commission reaffirms the goals aimed at reducing maternal and child mortality, combating HIV/AIDS and improving maternal health by 2015, as contained in the Millennium Development Goals, as well as the goal of achieving universal access to reproductive health, as set out at the International Conference on Population and Development, which are critical to the promotion of gender equality and the empowerment of women and girls.

13.　The Commission recalls the recognition in the Beijing Platform for Action of the role of the United Nations, including funds, programmes and specialized agencies, in particular the special roles of the United Nations Development Fund for Women (UNIFEM) and the International Research and Training Institute for the Advancement of Women (INSTRAW), within their respective mandates, and recognizes the role of the Office of the Special Adviser on Gender Issues and Advancement of Women and the Division for the Advancement of Women, as part of the United Nations system, in the promotion of gender equality and the empowerment of women and, therefore, in the implementation of the Platform for Action.

14.　The Commission also recalls that the Bretton Woods institutions, other financial institutions and the private sector also have an important role to play in ensuring that financing for development promotes gender equality and the empowerment of women and girls.

15.　The Commission recognizes the importance of non-governmental organizations, as well as other civil society actors, in advancing the implementation of the Beijing Declaration and Platform for Action.

16.　The Commission is concerned that insufficient political commitment and budgetary resources pose obstacles to promoting gender equality and women's empowerment and continue to undermine the effectiveness and sustainability of both national mechanisms for the advancement of women and women's organizations in advocating for, implementing, supporting and monitoring the effective implementation of the Beijing Declaration and Platform for Action and the outcome of the twenty-third special session of the General Assembly.

17.　The Commission is concerned about the growing feminization of poverty and reiterates that eradicating poverty is the greatest global challenge facing the world today, and an indispensable requirement for sustainable development, in particular for developing countries, including the least developed countries. In this regard, the Commission stresses that achieving the Millennium Development Goals and other internationally agreed development goals is a global effort that requires investing sufficient resources for gender equality and the empowerment of women and girls.

18.   The Commission remains concerned about the lingering negative consequences, including for women, of structural adjustment programmes, stemming from inappropriate design and application.

19.   The Commission expresses its concern about the under-resourcing in the area of gender equality in the United Nations system, including at UNIFEM and INSTRAW, the Office of the Special Adviser on Gender Issues and Advancement of Women and the Division for the Advancement of Women, and stresses the need for more effective tracking of resources allocated to and spent on enhancing gender equality and the empowerment of women across the United Nations system, including on gender mainstreaming.

20.   The Commission states that the global commitments for the achievement of gender equality and empowerment of women since the Fourth World Conference on Women, including through the Monterrey Consensus, have yet to be fully implemented.

21.   The Commission urges Governments and/or, as appropriate, the relevant funds, programmes and specialized agencies of the United Nations system, within their respective mandates, and invites the international financial institutions, civil society, non-governmental organizations and the private sector, bearing in mind national priorities, to take the following actions:

    (*a*)   Increase the investment in gender equality and the empower-ment of women and girls, taking into account the diversity of needs and circumstances of women and girls, including through mainstreaming a gender perspective in resource allocation and ensuring the necessary human, financial and material resources for specific and targeted activities to ensure gender equality at the local, national, regional and international levels, as well as through enhanced and increased international cooperation;

    (*b*)   Ensure that sufficient resources are allocated for activities target-ing the elimination of persistent obstacles to gender equality and the empowerment of women and girls in all critical areas of con-cern of the Platform for Action;

    (*c*)   Design and strengthen poverty eradication strategies, with the full and effective participation of women, that reduce the feminiza-tion of poverty and enhance the capacity of women and empower them to meet the negative social and economic impacts of globali-zation;

    (*d*)   Create an environment in which women and girls can fully share the benefits of the opportunities offered by globalization;

(e) Integrate a gender perspective into the design, implementation, monitoring and evaluation and reporting of all national economic policies, strategies and plans, in a coordinated manner across all policy areas, including in national development, social protection and poverty reduction strategies, and involve national mechanisms for the advancement of women and women's organizations in the design and development of such policies, strategies and plans with the goal of gender equality and the empowerment of women;

(f) Incorporate gender perspectives into all economic policymaking and increase the participation of women in economic governance structures and processes in order to ensure policy coherence and adequate resources for gender equality and the empowerment of women;

(g) Give priority to assisting the efforts of developing countries, including the least developed countries, to ensure the full and effective participation of women in deciding and implementing development strategies and integrating gender concerns into national programmes, including by providing adequate resources to operational activities for development in support of the efforts to achieve gender equality and the empowerment of women;

(h) Remove barriers and allocate adequate resources to enable the full representation and full and equal participation of women in political, social and economic decision-making and in administrative entities, in particular those responsible for economic and public finance policies, in order to guarantee the full and equal participation of women in the formulation of all plans, programmes and policies;

(i) Strengthen the capacities and mandates of institutional frameworks and accountability mechanisms, including of national machineries for the advancement of women, and ensure that they are continuously and adequately resourced and given the authority necessary to carry out their critical role in advocating for, supporting, monitoring and evaluating the integration of gender perspectives in all policy areas and the implementation of gender equality plans, programmes and legislation;

(j) Strengthen a coordinated and institutionalized dialogue between national mechanisms for the advancement of women, relevant governmental agencies and entities, including ministries of finance and planning and their gender focal points, and women's organizations in order to ensure the integration of gender perspectives into all national development policies, plans and budgets;

(k) Cost and adequately resource national policies, programmes, strategies and plans for gender equality and the empowerment of women, including gender mainstreaming and affirmative action strategies, and ensure that they are incorporated into overall national development strategies and reflected in relevant sector plans and budgets to achieve international and regional commitments for gender equality, including Millennium Development Goal 3;

(l) Allocate resources for capacity development in gender mainstreaming in all ministries, particularly within national women's machineries and finance ministries and, as appropriate, local authorities, in order to ensure that domestic resource mobilization and allocation are carried out in a gender-responsive manner, and reinforce national efforts in capacity-building in social and gender budget policies;

(m) Improve, systematize and fund the collection, analysis and dissemination of sex-disaggregated and gender-related data, including data disaggregated by age and other factors and data on women's contribution to the care economy, and develop necessary input, output and outcome indicators at all levels to measure progress in financing gender equality and the empowerment of women, in particular in introducing and implementing gender-responsive approaches to public finance;

(n) Undertake and disseminate gender analysis of policies and programmes related to macroeconomic stability, structural adjustment, external debt problems, taxation, investments, employment, markets and all relevant sectors of the economy and support and facilitate research in those areas, with a view to achieving the objectives of the Platform for Action and with respect to their impact on poverty, on inequality and particularly on women, as well as to assess their impact on family well-being and conditions and adjust them, as appropriate, to promote more equitable distribution of productive assets, wealth, opportunities, income and services;

(o) Carry out gender-sensitive analysis of revenues and expenditures in all policy areas and take into account the review and evaluation results in budget planning, allocation and revenue-raising in order to enhance the contribution of Government expenditures to accelerating the full and effective implementation of the Beijing Declaration and Platform for Action;

(p) Develop and implement, where appropriate, methodologies and tools, including national indicators, for gender-responsive planning and budgeting in order to incorporate gender perspectives systematically into budgetary policies at all levels, with a view to promoting gender equality in all policy areas;

(*q*) Urge developed countries that have not yet done so, in accordance with their commitments, to make concrete efforts towards meeting the target of 0.7 per cent of their gross national product for official development assistance to developing countries and 0.15 to 0.20 per cent of their gross national product to least developed countries, and encourage developing countries to build on the progress achieved in ensuring that official development assistance is used effectively to help meet development goals and targets and, inter alia, to assist them in achieving gender equality and the empowerment of women;

(*r*) Ensure the effective and equitable participation of developing countries in the formulation of financial standards and codes, with a view to the promotion of gender equality and the empowerment of women;

(*s*) Strengthen the focus and impact of development assistance, specifically targeting gender equality and empowerment of women and girls, in line with national development priorities, through both gender mainstreaming and funding of targeted activities and enhanced dialogue on those issues between donors and developing countries, and strengthen mechanisms to effectively measure resources allocated to incorporating gender perspectives in all sectors and thematic areas of development assistance;

(*t*) Encourage the integration of gender perspectives in aid modalities and efforts to enhance aid delivery mechanisms;

(*u*) Identify and implement development-oriented and durable solutions that integrate a gender perspective into the external debt and debt-servicing problems of developing countries, including least developed countries, inter alia, through debt relief, including the option of debt cancellation under official development assistance, in order to help them to finance programmes and projects targeted at development, including the advancement of women;

(*v*) Encourage international financial institutions to continue to take gender perspectives into account in the design of loans, grants, projects, programmes and strategies;

(*w*) Identify and address the differential impact of trade policies on women and men and incorporate gender perspectives in the formulation, implementation and evaluation of trade policies, develop strategies to expand trade opportunities for women producers and facilitate the active participation of women in national, regional and international trade decision-making structures and processes;

(x) Undertake gender-sensitive assessments of national labour laws, policies and programmes and establish gender-sensitive policies and guidelines for employment practices, including those of transnational corporations, building on appropriate multilateral instruments, including the conventions of the International Labour Organization;

(y) Allocate adequate resources for the elimination of all forms of discrimination against women in the workplace, including unequal access to labour market participation and wage inequalities, as well as reconciliation of work and private life for both women and men;

(z) Establish and fund active labour market policies devoted to the promotion of full and productive employment and decent work for all, including the full participation of women in all international and national development and poverty eradication strategies, the creation of more and better jobs for women, both urban and rural, and their inclusion in social protection and social dialogue;

(aa) Take measures to develop, finance, implement, monitor and evaluate gender-responsive policies and programmes aimed at promoting women's entrepreneurship and private initiative, including through microfinance, microcredit and cooperatives, and assist women-owned businesses in participating in and benefiting from, inter alia, international trade, technological innovation and transfer, investment and knowledge and skills training;

(bb) Fully maximize the role of and ensure access to microfinance tools, including microcredit for poverty eradication, employment generation and, especially, for the empowerment of women, encourage the strengthening of existing and emerging microcredit institutions and their capacities, including through the support of international financial institutions, and ensure that best practices are widely disseminated;

(cc) Undertake legislative and administrative reforms to give women full and equal access to economic resources, including the right to inheritance and to ownership of land and other property, credit, natural resources and appropriate technologies;

(dd) Take all appropriate measures to eliminate discrimination against women and increase their access to and control over bank loans, mortgages and other forms of financial credit, giving special attention to poor, uneducated women; support women's access to legal assistance; encourage the financial sector to mainstream gender perspectives in its policies and programmes; ensure women's full and equal access to training and productive resources and social protection; and facilitate equal access of women, particularly women in developing and least developed countries, to markets at all levels;

(*ee*) Strengthen education, health, and social services and effectively utilize resources to achieve gender equality and the empowerment of women and ensure women's and girls' rights to education at all levels and the enjoyment of the highest attainable standard of physical and mental health, including sexual and reproductive health, as well as quality, affordable and universally accessible health care and services, in particular primary health care;

(*ff*) Address the overall expansion and feminization of the HIV/AIDS pandemic, taking into account that women and girls bear a disproportionate share of the burden imposed by the HIV/AIDS crisis, that they are more easily infected, that they play a key role in care and that they have become more vulnerable to violence, stigma and discrimination, poverty and marginalization from their families and communities as a result of the HIV/AIDS crisis, and, in that regard, significantly scale up efforts towards the goal of universal access to comprehensive prevention programmes, treatment, care and support by 2010 and ensure that those efforts integrate and promote gender equality;

(*gg*) Ensure adequate financing for women's full, equal and effective participation at all levels in conflict prevention, management and resolution, peace negotiations and peacebuilding, including adequate national and international funding to ensure proper access to disarmament, demobilization and reintegration and other relevant programmes for women and girls;

(*hh*) Reduce excessive military expenditures, including global military expenditures, trade in arms and investment for arms production and acquisition, taking into consideration national security requirements, in order to permit the possible allocation of additional funds for social and economic development, including for gender equality and the advancement of women;

(*ii*) Ensure that adequate resources are allocated for activities targeting persistent serious obstacles to the advancement of women in situations of armed conflict and in conflicts of other types, wars of aggression, foreign occupation, colonial or other alien domination as well as terrorism;

(*jj*) Integrate a gender perspective into the design, implementation, monitoring, evaluation and reporting of national environmental policies, strengthen mechanisms and provide adequate resources to ensure women's full and equal participation in decision-making at all levels on environmental issues, in particular on strategies related to the impact of climate change on the lives of women and girls;

(kk) Strengthen coordination, accountability, effectiveness and efficiency in the United Nations system for the achievement of gender equality and the empowerment of women, including through more effective mainstreaming in all aspects and enhancing its capacity to assist States effectively, at their request, in implementing their programmes on gender equality and the empowerment of women and, to that end, make adequate and reliable human and financial resources available;

(ll) Create and enhance a supportive environment for the mobilization of resources by non-governmental organizations, in particular women's organizations and networks, to enable them to increase their effectiveness and to contribute to gender equality and the empowerment of women, including through assisting in the implementation of the Platform for Action and participating in policy processes and programme delivery;

(mm) Provide assistance to States parties to the Convention on the Elimination of All Forms of Discrimination against Women, upon their request, to support the implementation of the obligations of States parties under the Convention.

22. The Commission invites the Committee on the Elimination of Discrimination against Women to continue to give, while exercising its mandated functions, due consideration to financing for gender equality and the empowerment of women in its work.

23. The Commission requests Member States, with a view to strengthening financing for gender equality and the empowerment of women, to integrate gender perspectives in the preparations for and outcome of the Follow-up International Conference on Financing for Development to Review the Implementation of the Monterrey Consensus, to be held in Qatar in 2008.

Fifty-third session
2-13 March 2009

Agreed conclusions:

The equal sharing of responsibilities between women and men, including caregiving in the context of HIV/AIDS

The agreed conclusions adopted for the fifty-third session of the Commission on the Status of Women can be found in the *Official Records of the Economic and Social Council, 2009, Supplement No. 7* (E/2009/27-E/CN.6/2009/15).

Agreed conclusions
The equal sharing of responsibilities between women and men, including caregiving in the context of HIV/AIDS

1. The Commission on the Status of Women reaffirms the Beijing Declaration and Platform for Action, the outcome documents of the twenty-third special session of the General Assembly, and the declaration adopted by the Commission on the occasion of the tenth anniversary of the Fourth World Conference on Women.

2. The Commission reaffirms the outcomes of the 1994 International Conference on Population and Development, the 1995 World Summit for Social Development, the 2000 Millennium Summit, the 2002 World Summit on Children and the 2002 Monterrey Consensus on Financing for Development, recalls the 2005 World Summit, and recognizes that their full and effective implementation is essential to achieve the equal sharing of responsibilities between women and men, including caregiving in the context of HIV/AIDS.

3. The Commission reiterates that the Convention on the Elimination of All Forms of Discrimination against Women and the Convention on the Rights of the Child, and the Optional Protocols thereto, as well as other conventions and treaties, provide a legal framework and a comprehensive set of measures for the promotion of equal sharing of responsibilities between women and men.

4. The Commission reiterates the 2001 Declaration of Commitment on HIV/AIDS and the 2006 Political Declaration on HIV/AIDS, which, inter alia, expressed concern that gender inequality increases women's vulnerability to HIV/AIDS and the overall expansion and feminization of the pandemic, and also acknowledges that women and girls bear the disproportionate burden of caring for and supporting those infected and affected by HIV/AIDS.

5. The Commission duly notes the Workers with Family Responsibilities Convention, 1981 (Convention No. 156) of the International Labour Organization and its corresponding Recommendation (No. 165), which provide a framework for reconciling work and family responsibilities.

6. The Commission recognizes that gender inequalities still exist and are reflected in imbalances of power between women and men in all spheres of society. The Commission further recognizes that everyone benefits from gender equality and that the negative impacts of gender inequality are borne by society as a whole, and emphasizes, therefore, that men and boys, through

taking responsibility themselves and working jointly in partnership with women and girls, are essential to achieving the goals of gender equality, development and peace. The Commission recognizes the capacity of men and boys in bringing about changes in attitudes, relationships and access to resources and decision-making which are critical for the promotion of gender equality and the full enjoyment of all human rights by women.

7.   The Commission recognizes that the full integration of women into the formal economy, in particular, into economic decision-making, means changing the current gender-based division of labour into new economic structures where women and men enjoy equal treatment, pay and power, including sharing of paid and unpaid work.

8.   The Commission notes that the costs of unequal sharing of responsibilities include weaker labour market attachment for women (forgone jobs, shorter working hours, confinement to informal work, and lower wages), weaker access to social security benefits, and less time for education/training, leisure and self-care, and political activities.

9.   The Commission recognizes that caregiving work at the household, family and community levels includes the support and care of children, older persons, the sick, persons with disabilities, and caring associated with family kinship and community responsibilities, which is affected by factors such as size of household and number and age of children, with significant differences between developed and developing countries in the availability of infrastructure and services supporting caregiving. The Commission also recognizes that gender inequality and discrimination contribute to the continuing imbalance in the division of labour between women and men and perpetuate stereotypical perceptions of men and women. The Commission further recognizes that changes in demographics in ageing and youthful societies, and in the context of HIV/AIDS, have increased the need for, and scope of, care.

10.   The Commission further welcomes ongoing partnerships between stakeholders at all levels and the commitments on gender equality and HIV/AIDS announced at the 2008 high-level event on the Millennium Development Goals.

11.   The Commission expresses its deep concern over the negative impact of the global economic and financial crisis, which could hamper progress in achieving the Millennium Development Goals and the implementation of the Beijing Declaration and Platform for Action.

12.   The Commission acknowledges the important role of national machineries for the advancement of women, national human rights institutions where they exist, and civil society, especially women's organizations, in advancing the implementation of the Beijing Declaration and Platform for Action and in promoting the equal sharing of responsibilities between

women and men, and recognizes their contributions to the work of the Commission.

13.   The Commission reaffirms the commitment to the equal participation of women and men in public and political life as a key element in women's and men's equal participation in caregiving.

14.   The Commission acknowledges General Assembly resolution 62/277 of 15 September 2008, in particular its gender-specific provisions, and in this context encourages the ongoing work on gender equality and the empowerment of women.

15.   The Commission urges Governments, including local authorities, to take the following actions, as appropriate, with the relevant entities of the United Nations system, international and regional organizations, within their respective mandates, as well as civil society, the private sector, employer organizations, trade unions, media and other relevant actors:

   (*a*)   Intensify efforts to fully implement the Beijing Platform for Action, the outcome documents of the International Conference on Population and Development and the World Summit for Social Development, and the Monterrey Consensus on Financing for Development, and the outcomes of their follow-up processes;

   (*b*)   Consider ratifying or acceding to, as a particular matter of priority, the Convention on the Elimination of All Forms of Discrimination against Women, the Convention on the Rights of the Child and their respective Optional Protocols, limit the extent of any reservations that they lodge and regularly review such reservations with a view to withdrawing them so as to ensure that no reservation is incompatible with the object and purpose of the relevant treaty; and implement them fully by, inter alia, putting in place effective national legislation, policies and action plans;

   (*c*)   Consider, as a matter of priority, the ratification and implementation of the Workers with Family Responsibilities Convention, 1981 (Convention No. 156) of the International Labour Organization, and the implementation of its corresponding Recommendation (No. 165), which provide a framework for reconciling work and family responsibilities;

   (*d*)   Review, and, where appropriate, revise, amend or abolish all laws, regulations, policies, practices and customs that discriminate against women or have a discriminatory impact on women, and ensure that the provisions of multiple legal systems, where they exist, comply with international human rights obligations, commitments and principles, including the principle of non-discrimination;

(e) Ensure that women and children have full and equal access to effective legal protection against violations, including through domestic mechanisms of justice which are monitored and revised to ensure that they function without discrimination, as set out under all conventions related to human rights, including the Convention on the Elimination of All Forms of Discrimination against Women;

(f) Mainstream gender perspectives into all legislation, policies and programmes and promote incorporation of gender-responsive budgeting processes across all areas and at all levels, and enhance international cooperation to promote gender equality and empowerment of women and the equal sharing of responsibilities between women and men, including caregiving in the context of HIV/AIDS;

(g) Establish concrete goals and benchmarks and adopt positive actions and temporary special measures, as appropriate, to enhance women's equal participation in decision-making processes at all levels to further the equal sharing of responsibilities between women and men;

(h) Strengthen coordination, accountability, effectiveness and efficiency in the United Nations system, including its capacity to support Member States in the implementation of national policies for the achievement of, and to address under-resourcing in, gender equality and the empowerment of women;

(i) Promote understanding between women and men in order to strengthen women's access to resources and decision-making in policies and programmes to support caregiving, including in the context of HIV/AIDS. Ensure that men and boys, whose role is critical in achieving gender equality, are actively involved in policies and programmes that aim to improve the equal sharing of responsibilities with women and girls, so as to foster changes in attitudes and behaviour patterns in order to promote and protect the human rights of women and the girl child;

(j) Take appropriate measures to achieve equal sharing of work and parental responsibilities between women and men, including measures to reconcile care and professional life and emphasize men's equal responsibilities with respect to household work;

(k) Acknowledge the need to address violence against women holistically, including through the recognition of linkages between violence against women and other issues such as HIV/AIDS, poverty eradication, food security, peace and security, humanitarian assistance, health and crime prevention;

(*l*) Make efforts to devise comprehensive social and cultural strategies, including policies and programmes, that acknowledge the societal and individual value of adequate care for all and provide both women and men with full and equal human development opportunities;

(*m*) Take measures to protect and address the needs of women and girls in situations of humanitarian emergencies, in particular those carrying a disproportionate burden of caregiving responsibilities;

(*n*) Design, strengthen and implement national development plans and strategies, including poverty eradication strategies, with the full and effective participation of women and girls, including in decision-making, that reduce the feminization of poverty and HIV/AIDS, to enhance the capacity of women and girls and empower them to meet the negative social and economic impacts of globalization;

(*o*) Design, implement and promote family-friendly policies and services, including affordable, accessible and quality care services for children and other dependants, parental and other leave schemes and campaigns to sensitize public opinion and other relevant actors on equal sharing of employment and family responsibilities between women and men;

(*p*) Promote greater understanding and recognition that caregiving is a critical societal function and should be equally shared between women and men within the family and households, and strengthen dialogue and coordination between all relevant stakeholders;

(*q*) Measure, in quantitative and qualitative terms, unremunerated work that is outside national accounts, in order better to reflect its value in such accounts, and recognize and take necessary measures to incorporate the value and cost of unpaid work within and between households and society at large in policies, strategies, plans and budgets across all relevant sectors;

(*r*) Measure, in quantitative terms, unremunerated work that is outside national accounts, to assess and reflect its value accurately in satellite or other official accounts that are separate from but consistent with core national accounts;

(*s*) Adopt, implement and monitor gender-sensitive policies and programmes to ensure the full enjoyment of human rights, social protection, and decent working conditions of both paid and unpaid caregivers;

(*t*)   Adopt, implement, evaluate and, where necessary, review gender-sensitive legislation and policies that promote balance between paid work and family responsibilities, reduce occupational and sectoral segregation, advance equal remuneration, and ensure that workers with flexible arrangements are not discriminated against;

(*u*)   Ensure that women and men have access to maternity, paternity, parental and/or other forms of leave, and consider providing incentives to men to avail themselves of such leave for caregiving purposes, and take measures to protect women and men against dismissal, and guarantee their right to resume the same or equivalent post after utilizing such leave;

(*v*)   Ensure that social protection measures such as health insurance, child and family allowances and information on these benefits are widely available and accessible, and that these measures do not reinforce gender biases, that workers are not discriminated against when they avail themselves of the benefits available, and that these benefits are regularly reviewed to target all workers, including, as appropriate, in the informal sector;

(*w*)   Develop and improve sustainable and adequate social protection and/or insurance schemes, including pension and savings schemes, that meet basic minimum needs, and recognize leave periods for caregiving in the calculation of respective benefits;

(*x*)   Strengthen efforts to protect the rights and ensure decent work conditions for all domestic workers, including women migrant domestic workers, in, inter alia, their working hours and wages, and to improve their access to health-care services and other social and economic benefits;

(*y*)   Take measures to address the special needs of girls, including migrant girls, employed as domestic workers and caregivers, as well as those that have to perform excessive domestic chores and caregiving responsibilities, and to provide access to education, vocational training, health services, food, shelter and recreation, while ensuring the prevention and elimination of child labour and economic exploitation of girls;

(*z*)   Develop gender-sensitive measures, including national action plans, where appropriate, to eliminate the worst forms of child labour;

(*aa*)   Strengthen education, health and social services and effectively utilize resources to achieve gender equality and the empowerment of women and ensure women's and girls' rights to education at all levels and the enjoyment of the highest attainable standard of physical and mental health, including sexual and reproductive health, as well as quality, affordable and universally accessible primary health care and services, as well as sex education based on full and accurate information in a manner consistent with the evolving capacities of girls and boys, and with appropriate direction and guidance;

(*bb*) Develop and/or expand, and adequately resource, the provision of equitable, quality, accessible and affordable care and support services for all people needing care, including through community-based support systems, while ensuring that such services meet the needs of both caregivers and care recipients, bearing in mind the increased labour mobility of women and men, and, where applicable, kinship and extended family responsibilities, and the importance of adequate nutrition;

(*cc*) Assess and respond to the needs for integrated human resources at all levels of the health system, in order to achieve Millennium Development Goal 6 and the targets of the Declaration of Commitment on HIV/AIDS and the Political Declaration on HIV/AIDS, and take actions, as appropriate, to effectively govern the recruitment, training, deployment and retention of skilled health personnel in prevention, treatment, care and support for those infected and affected by HIV/AIDS;

(*dd*) Ensure that adequate investments are made to strengthen efforts through, inter alia, the allocation of resources to provide quality, accessible and affordable public services, including education, health and other social services which incorporate gender equality as a basic principle;

(*ee*) Increase the availability, access to, and use of critical public infrastructure, such as transportation, the provision of a safe, reliable and clean water supply, sanitation, energy, telecommunications and affordable housing programmes, in particular in poverty-stricken and rural areas, to reduce the burden of care on households;

(*ff*) Significantly scale up efforts towards the goal of universal access to comprehensive HIV/AIDS prevention programmes, treatment, care and support by 2010, and the goal of halting and reversing the spread of HIV/AIDS by 2015, and ensure that those efforts promote gender equality and take into account the caregiving responsibilities of both women and men;

(*gg*) Reaffirm that the full realization of all human rights and fundamental freedoms for all is an essential element of the global response to the HIV/AIDS pandemic, and ensure that in all national policies and programmes designed to provide comprehensive HIV/AIDS prevention, treatment, care and support, particular attention and support is given to women and girls at risk of, infected with or affected by HIV/AIDS, including young and adolescent mothers, and recognize that, inter alia, preventing and reducing stigma and discrimination, eradicating poverty and mitigating the impact of underdevelopment are critical elements to achieve the internationally agreed goals in this regard;

(*hh*) Reaffirm that access to medication in the context of pandemics, such as HIV/AIDS, is one of the fundamental elements to achieve progressively the full realization of the right of everyone to the enjoyment of the highest attainable standard of physical and mental health;

(*ii*) Recognize the increased feminization of the HIV/AIDS pandemic and ensure that existing HIV/AIDS policies, strategies, resources and programmes at all levels are reviewed and adapted to ensure that they contribute to empowering women and reducing their vulnerability to HIV/AIDS;

(*jj*) Integrate gender perspectives into national HIV/AIDS policies and programmes, as well as into national monitoring and evaluation systems, taking into account the caregiving responsibilities of both women and men, including in community, family and home-based care, and ensure the full and active participation of caregivers, in particular women, including those living with HIV/AIDS, in decision-making processes;

(*kk*) Develop multisectoral policies and programmes and identify, strengthen and take all necessary measures to address the needs of women and girls, including older women and widows, infected with or affected by HIV/AIDS, and those providing unpaid care, especially women and girls heading households, for, inter alia, social and legal protection, increased access to financial and economic resources including microcredit and sustainable economic opportunities, education including opportunities to continue education, as well as access to health services, including affordable antiretroviral treatment and nutritional support;

(*ll*) Emphasize the importance of HIV prevention as a long-term strategy to reduce the number of new HIV infections and, consequently, to reduce the burden of caregiving responsibilities on both women and men through universal access to comprehensive prevention, treatment, care and support programmes, including sexual and reproductive health and services, and to increase access to voluntary and confidential counselling and HIV testing, investments in HIV/AIDS and sex education and awareness, based on full and accurate information in a manner consistent with the evolving capacities of the child, with appropriate direction and guidance, research and development of, and access to, new, safe, quality and affordable HIV/AIDS prevention products, diagnostics, medicines and treatment commodities, including female-controlled methods, and new preventive technologies and microbicides and AIDS vaccines;

(*mm*) Strengthen, expand, improve and promote the accessibility of quality comprehensive public health care and services, including community-based health services specifically related to the prevention and treatment of HIV/AIDS, including for people with disabilities, as well as hospital and hospice-based care, and psychosocial support services, and increase the number of professional health-care providers, especially in rural areas, to alleviate the current burden on women and girls who provide unpaid care services in the context of HIV/AIDS;

(*nn*) Design and implement programmes, including awareness-raising programmes, to promote the active involvement of men and boys in eliminating gender stereotypes as well as gender inequality and gender-based violence and abuse, and educate men, including young men, to understand their role and responsibility in the spread of HIV/AIDS and in matters related to their sexuality, reproduction, child-rearing and the promotion of equality between women and men and girls and boys, and enable women and men to adopt safe and responsible, non-coercive sexual and reproductive behaviour, including increased access to an appropriate and comprehensive package of prevention programmes and support, to prevent the transmission of HIV and other sexually transmitted infections, including through increased access to education, including in the areas of sexual and reproductive health, for young people, and encourage the full participation of men and boys in caregiving, prevention, treatment, support and impact evaluation programmes;

(*oo*) Develop and implement appropriate policies and programmes to address stereotypical attitudes and behaviours to promote the equal sharing of responsibilities between women and men across the life cycle;

(*pp*) Develop gender-sensitive education and training programmes, including for educators at all levels, aimed at eliminating discriminatory attitudes towards women and girls and men and boys, to address gender stereotypes in the context of equal sharing of responsibilities between women and men, including caregiving in the context of HIV/AIDS;

(*qq*) Take measures to increase the participation of men in caregiving both within households and in care professions, such as information and awareness campaigns, education and training, school curriculum, peer programmes and government policies to promote men's participation and responsibilities as fathers and caregivers, and to encourage men and boys to become agents of change in promoting the human rights of women and in challenging gender stereotypes, in particular as they relate to men's roles in parenting and infant development;

(*rr*) Address gender stereotypes in the context of equal sharing of responsibilities between women and men by encouraging media to promote gender equality and the non-stereotypical portrayal of women and girls and men and boys, and by carrying out and publishing research on views, especially of men and boys, on gender equality and perceptions of gender roles, as well as by assessing the impact of efforts undertaken in achieving gender equality;

(*ss*) Develop strategies to eliminate gender stereotypes in all spheres of life, including in public and political life, and foster the positive portrayal of women and girls as leaders and decision makers at all levels and in all areas, to achieve the equal sharing of responsibilities between women and men;

(*tt*) Encourage and support men and boys to take an active part in the prevention and elimination of all forms of violence, especially gender-based violence, including by developing strategies to eliminate gender stereotypes and by developing programmes that promote respectful relationships, and rehabilitate perpetrators as part of a strategy of zero tolerance for violence against women and girls;

(*uu*) Conduct research and collect sex- and age-disaggregated data and develop gender-sensitive indicators, as appropriate, to inform policymaking, conduct assessments in a coordinated manner, and measure progress in the sharing of responsibilities between women and men, including in the context of HIV/AIDS, and identify the obstacles and stereotypes men may face in assuming increased caregiving responsibilities;

(*vv*) Strengthen the capacity of national statistical offices and, when necessary, measurement systems, to effectively collect comprehensive information on all categories of activities, including through time-use surveys, to inform policy development that facilitates the sharing of unpaid work between women and men;

(*ww*) Enhance the collection and dissemination of statistics on the relative participation of women and men in leadership roles in public office and in strategic economic, social and political decision-making positions, in order to promote the equal sharing of responsibilities between women and men in these spheres;

(*xx*) Adopt appropriate measures to overcome negative impacts of the economic and financial crisis, including on women and girls, and integrate a gender perspective into these measures so that they equally benefit women and men, while seeking to maintain whenever possible adequate levels of funding for gender equality and the empowerment of women;

(*yy*) Take all appropriate measures to integrate women, on an equal basis with men, in decision-making regarding sustainable resource management and the development of policies and programmes for sustainable development, including to address the disproportionate impact of climate change on women, including their displacement from income-generating activities, which greatly adds to unremunerated work, such as caregiving, and negatively impacts on their health, well-being and quality of life, particularly those whose livelihoods and daily subsistence depend directly on sustainable ecosystems;

(*zz*) Allocate adequate financial resources at the international level for the implementation of the Beijing Platform for Action, the Cairo Plan of Action, the outcome documents of the twenty-third special session of the General Assembly, the Declaration of Commitment on HIV/AIDS and the Political Declaration on HIV/AIDS, in developing countries, especially through the strengthening of their national capacities;

(*aaa*) Strengthen international cooperation in order to assist in the development of human resources for health, through technical assistance and training, as well as to increase universal access to health services, including in remote and rural areas, taking into account the challenges facing developing countries in the retention of skilled health personnel;

(*bbb*) Urge developed countries that have not yet done so, in accordance with their commitments, to make concrete efforts towards meeting the target of 0.7 per cent of their gross national product for official development assistance to developing countries and 0.15 to 0.20 per cent of their gross national product to least developed countries, and encourage developing countries to build on the progress achieved in ensuring that official development assistance is used effectively to help meet development goals and targets and, inter alia, to assist them in achieving gender equality and the empowerment of women.

The Bureau of the Commission on the Status of Women, 1996-2009

Fortieth session

Ms. **Sharon Brennan-Haylock** (Bahamas), Chairperson

Ms. **Ljudmila Boskova** (Bulgaria), Vice-Chairperson

Ms. **Rafika Khouini** (Tunisia), Vice-Chairperson

Ms. **Karin Stoltenberg** (Norway), Vice-Chairperson

Ms. **Sweeya Santipitaks** (Thailand), Vice-Chairperson

Forty-first session

Ms. **Sharon Brennen-Haylock** (Bahamas), Chairperson

Ms. **Ljudmila Boskova** (Bulgaria), Vice-Chairperson

Ms. **Zakia Amara Bouaziz** (Tunisia), Vice-Chairperson*

Ms. **Eva Hildrum** (Norway), Vice-Chairperson**

Ms. **Sweeya Santipitaks** (Thailand), Vice-Chairperson

Forty-second and forty-third sessions

Ms. **Patricia Flor** (Germany), Chairperson

Mr. **Karam Fadi Habib** (Lebanon), Vice-Chairperson

Ms. **Marcela Maria Nicodemos** (Brazil), Vice-Chairperson

Ms. **Nonhlanhla P. L. Mlangeni** (Swaziland), Vice-Chairperson

Ms. **Zuzana Vranová** (Slovakia), Vice-Chairperson

Forty-fourth and forty-fifth sessions

Ms. **Dubravka Šimonović** (Croatia), Chairperson

Ms. **Kirsten Geelan** (Denmark), Vice-Chairperson

Ms. **Misako Kaji** (Japan), Vice-Chairperson***

Ms. **Loreto Leyton** (Chile), Vice-Chairperson

---

*   Elected to replace Ms. Rafika Khouini (Tunisia).

**   Elected to replace Ms. Karin Stoltenberg (Norway).

*** Resigned after forty-fourth session.

Mr. **Mankeur Ndiaye** (Senegal), Vice-Chairperson

Ms. **Atsuko Nishimura** (Japan), Vice-Chairperson*

Forty-sixth and forty-seventh sessions

H.E. Mr. **Othman Jerandi** (Tunisia), Chairperson

Mr. **Fernando Estellita Lins de Salvo Coimbra** (Brazil),
Vice-Chairperson

Ms. **Kyung-wha Kang** (Republic of Korea), Vice-Chairperson

Ms. **Birgit Stevens** (Belgium), Vice-Chairperson

Ms. **Lala Imrahimova** (Azerbijan), Vice-Chairperson

Forty-eighth session

Ms. **Kyung-wha Kang** (Republic of Korea), Chairperson

Ms. **Lala Ibrahimova** (Azerbaijan), Vice-Chairperson**

Ms. **Tebatso Future Baleseng** (Botswana), Vice-Chairperson

Ms. **Beatrice Maille** (Canada), Vice-Chairperson

Ms. **Carmen-Rosa Arias** (Peru), Vice-Chairperson

Forty-ninth session

Ms. **Kyung-wa Kang** (Republic of Korea), Chairperson

Ms. **Marine Davtyan** (Republic of Armenia), Vice-Chairperson***

Ms. **Tebatso Future Baleseng** (Botswana), Vice-Chairperson

Ms. **Beatrice Maille** (Canada), Vice-Chairperson

Ms. **Romy Tincopa** (Peru), Vice-Chairperson****

Fiftieth session

H.E. Ms. **Carmen María Gallardo** (El Salvador), Chairperson

Ms. **Szilvia Szabo** (Hungary), Vice-Chairperson

Mrs. **Adekunbi Abibat Sonaike** (Nigeria), Vice-Chairperson

---

*   Elected to replace Ms. Misako Kaji during the forty-fifth session.

**   Elected for a term of one year.

***   Elected for a term of one year.

**** Elected to replace Ms. Carmen-Rosa Arias (Peru).

Mr. Thomas Woodroffe (United Kingdom), Vice-Chairperson

Mr. Dicky Komar (Indonesia), Vice-Chairperson-cum-Rapporteur

Fifty-first session

H.E. Ms. Carmen María Gallardo (El Salvador), Chairperson

Mrs. Adekunbi Abibat Sonaike (Nigeria), Vice-Chairperson

Mr. Thomas Woodroffe (United Kingdom), Vice-Chairperson

Mr. Balázs Csuday (Hungary), Vice-Chairperson*

Mr. Dicky Komar (Indonesia), Vice-Chairperson-cum-Rapporteur

Fifty-second and fifty-third sessions

H.E. Mr. Olivier Belle (Belgium), Chairperson

Mr. Ara Margarian (Armenia), Vice-Chairperson

Ms. Enna Park (Republic of Korea), Vice-Chairperson

Mr. Julio Peralta (Paraguay), Vice-Chairperson

Ms. Cécile Mballa Eyenga (Cameroon), Vice-Chairperson-cum-Rapporteur

---

*   Elected to replace Ms. Szilvia Szabo (Hungary).

Annex II
Expert Group Meetings organized by the Division for the Advancement of Women on the themes under consideration by the Commission on the Status of Women[105]

Forty-first session

Vocational training and lifelong learning of women
(Turin, Italy, 2-6 December 1996)

Women, population and sustainable development: The road from Rio, Cairo and Beijing
(Santo Domingo, Dominican Republic, 18-22 November 1996)

Women and economic decision-making in international financial institutions and transnational corporations
(Boston, United States of America, 11-15 November 1996)

Forty-second session

Adolescent girls and their rights
(Addis Ababa, Ethiopia, 13-17 October 1997)

Gender-based persecution
(Toronto, Canada, 9-12 November 1997)

Promoting women's enjoyment of their economic and social rights
(Abo/Turku, Finland, 1-4 December 1997)

Ageing women and care
(Valletta, Malta, 30 November–2 December 1997)

Forty-third session

Women and health: mainstreaming the gender perspective into the health sector
(Tunis, Tunisia, 28 September–2 October 1998)

---

[105]   The reports of the Expert Group Meetings are available at http://www.un.org/womenwatch/daw/documents/egm.htm.

National machineries for gender equality
(Santiago, Chile, 31 August–4 September 1998)

Forty-fifth session

The AIDS pandemic and its gender implications
(Windhoek, Namibia, 13-17 November 2000)

Gender and racial discrimination
(Zagreb, Croatia, 21-24 November 2000)

Forty-sixth session

Empowerment of women through the life cycle as a transformative strategy for poverty eradication
(New Delhi, India, 26-29 November 2001)

Environmental management and the mitigation of natural disasters: a gender perspective
(Ankara, Turkey, 6-9 November 2001)

Forty-seventh session

Trafficking in women and girls
(Glen Cove, United States of America, 18-22 November 2002)

Participation and access of women to the media and their impact on and use as an instrument for the advancement and empowerment of women
(Beirut, Lebanon, 12-15 November 2002)

Information and communication technologies and their impact on and use as an instrument for the advancement and empowerment of women
(Seoul, Republic of Korea, 11-14 November 2002)

Forty-eighth session

Peace agreements as a means for promoting gender equality and ensuring participation of women—A framework of model provisions
(Ottawa, Canada, 10-13 November 2003)

The role of men and boys in achieving gender equality

(Brasilia, Brazil, 21-24 October 2003)

Fiftieth session

Equal participation of women and men in decision-making processes, with special emphasis on political participation and leadership

(Addis Ababa, Ethiopia, 24-27 October 2005)

Enhancing participation of women in development through an enabling environment for achieving gender equality and the advancement of women

(Bangkok, Thailand, 8-11 November 2005)

Fifty-first session

Elimination of all forms of discrimination and violence against the girl child

(Florence, Italy, 25-28 September 2006)

Fifty-second session

Financing for gender equality and the empowerment of women

(Oslo, Norway, 4-7 September 2007)

Fifty-third session

The equal sharing of responsibilities between women and men, including caregiving in the context of HIV/AIDS

(Geneva, Switzerland, 6-9 October 2008)